The I Ching For Managers & Leaders

The
I Ching
For Managers & Leaders

Ancient wisdom for modern leaders

John Rodwell

The wisest, most ethical decision making tool in history.
For the times when you need some guidance

© John Rodwell 2015

All rights reserved. No part of this book may be used or reproduced in any manner whatsoever without written permission.

Published 2015 by Lulu.com

ISBN: 978-1-326-23650-2

Also Available

Keep a record of all your major I Ching consultations with this tailor made Journal.

ISBN 978-1-326-20993-3

See next page for content and layout

I CHING JOURNAL ENTRY

Date:			Area:	

Issue / Problem / Question for the Oracle

Line No.	Reading 1	Reading 2 (If Changes)
6		
5		
4		
3		
2		
1		
Chapter		

Changes	1	2	3	4	5	6

Reflections on the reading(s)

Action Planned

Consequences / Other Notes

Contents

INTRODUCTION 1
PRINCIPLES OF THE I CHING 2
CONSULTING THE I CHING - THE THREE COIN
METHOD 4
YOUR I CHING READING 6
CHAPTER TABLE 7
THE I CHING CHAPTERS 1 - 64 9
1. THE CREATIVE 10
2. THE RECEPTIVE 12
3. DIFFICULTY AT THE BEGINNING 14
4. YOUTHFUL FOLLY 16
5. WAITING 18
6. CONFLICT 20
7. THE ARMY 22
8. HOLDING TOGETHER 24
9. THE TAMING POWER OF THE SMALL 26
10. TREADING 28
11. PEACE 30
12. STANDSTILL 32
13. FELLOWSHIP 34
14. POSESSION IN GREAT MEASURE 36
15. MODESTY 38
16. ENTHUSIASM 40

17. FOLLOWING 42
18. REMOVING DECAY 44
19. APPROACH 46
20. CONTEMPLATION 48
21. BITING THROUGH 50
22. GRACE 52
23. SPLITTING APART 54
24. RETURN 56
25. INNOCENCE 58
26. THE TAMING POWER OF THE GREAT 60
27. PROVIDING NOURISHMENT 62
28. GREAT HEAVINESS 64
29. THE ABYSMAL 66
30. THE CLINGING 68
31. INFLUENCE 70
32. DURATION 72
33. RETREAT 74
34. THE POWER OF THE GREAT 76
35. PROGRESS 78
36. DARKENING OF THE LIGHT 80
37. THE FAMILY 82
38. OPPOSITION 84
39. OBSTRUCTION 86
40. DELIVERANCE 88
41. DECREASE 90

42. INCREASE 92
43. BREAKTHROUGH 94
44. COMING TO MEET 96
45. GATHERING TOGETHER 98
46. PUSHING UPWARD 100
47. OPPRESSION 102
48. THE WELL 104
49. REVOLUTION 106
50. THE GREAT BOWL 108
51. THE AROUSING 110
52. KEEPING STILL 112
53. DEVELOPMENT 114
54. THE MARRYING MAIDEN 116
55. ABUNDANCE 118
56. THE WANDERER 120
57. THE GENTLE 122
58. THE JOYOUS 124
59. DISPERSION 126
60. LIMITATION 128
61. INNER TRUTH 130
62. GREAT SMALLNESS 132
63. AFTER COMPLETION 134
64. BEFORE COMPLETION 136

INTRODUCTION

Welcome to the oracle of the I Ching (pronounced Yee-King) the ancient Chinese oracle: 'The Book of Changes'.

Today's working life is changing all the time. Organisations are looking for managers and leaders who can bring the best out of their people. In times of austerity, recession and having to 'do more with less'; this is no easy task. The I Ching however, can help.

The I Ching has been around for over 3,000 years. Amazingly it is just as powerful today as it has been throughout the millennia.

The I Ching is not magic. It is not from the realm of the occult and neither is it for the superstitious or gullible. It is instead a way of enabling anyone with a receptive mind to see their personal situation reflected in the images that the oracle provides.

The oracle enables those who look, to see their circumstances in a new light. It provides a truly moral way of going forward, neither too strongly, nor too weakly but in harmony and balance with the time.

The I Ching is a work of Eastern philosophy that resonates well with the Western mind. The oracle itself has no power. The power comes from the psyche of the reader who can intuitively understand the meaning within the words.

PRINCIPLES OF THE I CHING

Yin and Yang

The I Ching is an oracle to be consulted to answer important questions in our lives; at work and at home. It is based on the principle of opposing forces: light and dark; weak and strong; good and evil.

In the I Ching the gentle, receptive, flexible 'female' force is characterised as Yin. The strong, forceful, active 'male' force is characterised by Yang.

The I Ching describes the benefits of maintaining an appropriate balance between our use of the Yin and Yang forces. The balance does not always have to be equal, but it must always be in harmony with the situation we find ourselves in.

Too much Yang can lead to arrogance, aggression, haste and intolerance. Too much Yin can lead to excessive passivity, blind obedience and exploitation.

Trigrams and Hexagrams

In the I Ching, Yin and Yang forces are expressed as lines. Yin is a broken line. Yang is a solid line.

The basic symbolic unit is a Trigram made up of three lines. Each Trigram has a name and an association as you will see overleaf.

HEAVEN (The Creative)	☰
EARTH (The Receptive)	☷
THUNDER (The Arousing)	☳
WATER (The Abysmal)	☵
MOUNTAIN (Keeping still)	☶
WIND / WOOD (The Gentle)	☴
FIRE (The Clinging)	☲
LAKE (The Joyous)	☱

Pairing these Trigrams gives 64 Hexagrams which also have their own names. These Hexagrams form the basis of an I Ching reading.

What to consult about

The I Ching should be consulted on issues and questions that are important in your role as a manager and leader. It should be consulted when you need to obtain some insight into a situation that is affecting you and obtain some guidance on how to deal with it.

You can think of a general issue like 'The reorganisation at work' or ask a more specific question like 'What can I do about my team's morale?'

The I Ching shouldn't be used for superficial questions like: 'What shoes shall I wear today?', nor for questions requiring simple yes / no answers.

CONSULTING THE I CHING - THE THREE COIN METHOD

A common method to consult the I Ching is the three coin method. Three coins are thrown at the same time.

When they land, the heads (H) and tails (T) represent the lines that will build the Trigrams and the Hexagram:

H H H	Moving Yang	——⊖——
T T T	Moving Yin	—— ✕ ——
H H T	Yang	————————
T T H	Yin	—— ——

The coins are thrown six times in all to make the Hexagram made up of the two Trigrams. The process always starts at the bottom and works upwards.

Changes and Moving Lines

Whenever a 'Moving' Yin or Yang line is thrown, its opposite will also apply to your situation and you will have **two** Hexagrams to read.

The moving lines also indicate which 'Changes' will apply to your first reading. If you have moving lines in position numbers 2 and 4 for example, the Changes numbered 2 & 4 will apply to your reading as in the example below.

	1st Reading		2nd Reading
6	— —		— —
5	———		———
4	——O——	C4	— —
3	———		———
2	—X—	C2	———
1	———		— —

This example shows the first reading Hexagram, the Changes that apply and the second reading Hexagram which show how your situation may develop further into the future.

YOUR I CHING READING

This is what you will see when a Hexagram page is opened.

THE CONDITION
A description of what the Hexagram represents

THE JUDGEMENT
A judgement on the nature of the situation and what action you can take to achieve the most favourable outcome

THE IMAGE
How the situation relates to the natural world and/or what a 'Wise Leader' would do

After each Hexagram page is a page to show:

THE CHANGES
The Changes that may apply to your reading (numbered 1 - 6).

CHAPTER TABLE

After throwing your coins and drawing your Upper and Lower Trigrams, you can use the table below to find the relevant chapter numbers for your readings

		UPPER TRIGRAM							
L O W E R T R I G R A M		1	11	34	5	26	9	14	43
		12	2	16	8	23	20	35	45
		25	24	51	3	27	42	21	17
		6	7	40	29	4	59	64	47
		33	15	62	39	52	53	56	31
		44	46	32	48	18	57	50	28
		13	36	55	63	22	37	30	49
		10	19	54	60	41	61	38	58
		CHAPTER NUMBERS							

Remember, the Changes will only apply to your first reading, not your second.

THE I CHING
CHAPTERS 1 - 64

1. THE CREATIVE

Above: The Creative (Heaven)
Below: The Creative (Heaven)

THE CONDITION

This hexagram represents heaven the creative power. It is Yang: active, masculine, light giving, strong and firm. On earth it is represented by the actions of the Wise Leader who awakens the higher nature of others. The Creative is made apparent only through the effects of such activity.

THE JUDGEMENT

Success will be achieved through perseverance and patience. The Wise Leader understands the meaning of time: how it is the instrument of the Creative; and how it shapes and develops all beings in accord with their true natures. The Wise Leader knows what is enduring and what is transitory, and acts in the knowledge that each end is a new beginning.

THE IMAGE

As one day follows the next, the Creative never stops nor falters. The Wise Leader is steadfast in the aim of developing their influence and creating order and peace for all around them.

1. THE CREATIVE

CHANGES

1. Be patient and calm and show the strength of patience. Do not expend your powers prematurely. The time is not yet right.

2. Let your influence begin to be felt. Not by your rank or position, but by your strength of purpose. It should be effortless.

3. Now you need inner stability to counterbalance the fame that your influence brings. Beware of your integrity being consumed by ambition

4. There is a choice to be made - worldly importance, or spiritual growth and solitude. Be true to yourself and choose without blame.

5. Be in accord with the universe and your influence will spread everywhere. Go where you feel most comfortable, where you know you belong.

6. Climb too high and you will become isolated and lose touch with others. Beware of having aspirations beyond your powers.

2. THE RECEPTIVE

Above: The Receptive (Earth)
Below: The Receptive (Earth)

THE CONDITION

This hexagram represents the earth. It is primal Yin: yielding, gentle, dark, maternal, flexible and submissive. It is not the opposite of the Creative, it complements it. While the creative initiates things, the Receptive brings them into form.

THE JUDGEMENT

The nature of the Receptive is to follow with devotion. Don't strive to achieve everything. Be receptive to the influences of others. Success comes through being open and embracing all. Forcefulness can lead to evil, but you can still be strong, like the mare roaming the plains, tireless, strong and devoted. Follow. Do not try to lead lest you lose yourself.

THE IMAGE

The earth is huge, it carries all things upon it, good and bad. By inner strength the Wise Leader can carry all things without being swayed by them, and is open to all things that cross their path.

2. THE RECEPTIVE

CHANGES

1. Beware of the beginnings of failure, disappointment or evil. Nip it in the bud before it grows.

2. With calmness and tolerance accept all people equally. Act naturally and do what is self-evidently right. Be consistent and true, without self-doubt.

3. Conceal your abilities and let them mature unseen until the time is right. Work with restraint. Seek a deeper satisfaction from work than worldly goods and high rank

4. Be cautious, and steer clear of trying to stand above others. It can lead to anger or misunderstanding. Stay in the background where there is no praise, and no blame.

5. Your genuineness and your gracefulness come from within. You do not need to prove it overtly. Be discreet, that is where true success lies.

6. Do not reach for a position to which you are not entitled. Do not make an unnatural contest between Yin and Yang, dark and light. Both sides will suffer.

3. DIFFICULTY AT THE BEGINNING

Above: The Abysmal (Water)
Below: The Arousing (Thunder)

THE CONDITION

This hexagram represents thunder and rain. There is teeming chaos. It is like attending at the birth of a first child that is fraught with difficulties. But then, like a thunderstorm, it blows over. The tension is released and the air becomes fresh and clear again.

THE JUDGEMENT

The time of early growth is a difficult one. The dangers are many but there is the prospect of success. When things are still young and unformed, beware of acting too quickly. The Wise Leader holds back and also seeks the help of others rather than face the storms alone. Work with them, but do not rely wholly upon them. The chaos will pass and order will follow.

THE IMAGE

Clouds and rain and thunder are natural and are to be expected. The Wise Leader makes arrangements and organises things in that knowledge and works to bring order out of chaos.

3. DIFFICULTY AT THE BEGINNING

CHANGES

1. If you are hindered at the start of an enterprise, do not force your way forward. Keep your goal in sight and seek help from others. Avoid arrogance in doing so and you will find the right people.

2. Be cautious about help offered from an unexpected source. Do not commit yourself to anything. Bide your time

3. You must face your difficulties, but do not act hastily. Without the necessary guidance you should hold back rather than risk failure.

4. Despite the dangers, sometimes you just have to act. The first step is one that has to be taken. Taking shows inner clarity. There is no disgrace in accepting help from the right people.

5. Work through the difficulties step by step. If your helpers don't understand what you want, don't force things. Just keep working at it until the cloud lifts.

6. Sometimes you get stuck, cannot resolve the chaos and give up. It is sad, but aim to make a quick clean break and start anew.

4. YOUTHFUL FOLLY

Above: Keeping still (Mountain)
Below: The Abysmal (Water)

THE CONDITION

This hexagram represents immaturity and inexperience rather than stupidity. There is confusion here, like water gushing up from a spring not knowing where to go. There is also danger present, like being on the edge of an abyss. Yet out of this perplexity can come enlightenment.

THE JUDGEMENT

You could be the youth or the teacher. The youth needs to seek out the teacher and humbly acknowledge their lack of experience. The teacher must wait to be asked and then offer clear answers to help the youth decide. What is good in the youth must be strengthened, step by step, and with perseverance.

THE IMAGE

The mountain spring avoids stagnation by filling all hollow places. The Wise Leader, by being thorough, attains the clarity of a mountain spring and like the mountain achieves calmness at the edge of the abyss.

4. YOUTHFUL FOLLY

CHANGES

1. You may need to enforce discipline at the beginning. And ensure that the seriousness of the situation is acknowledged. As self discipline grows, you can gradually loosen the reins.

2. Be patient with the folly of youth. Tolerate shortcomings with kindness. Use your inner strength, rather than your external power to achieve this.

3. Wait to be asked for help with dignity and detachment. Do not throw yourself into service, it will help no-one.

4. If the youth is hopelessly entangled in a world of fantasy and irrational imaginings leave them to it. They will find out their folly in due course. Their humiliation can rescue them.

5. The youth who seeks guidance openly and with respect is on the right path. Help and enlightenment come to those who are ready to listen.

6. If punishment is necessary, it must not be given in anger but with the sole objective of restoring peace or preventing disorder.

5. WAITING

Above: The Abysmal (Water)
Below: The Creative (Heaven)

THE CONDITION

These two Trigrams represent inner strength in the face of danger. This strength does not plunge ahead. It bides its time. It is weakness that does not have the patience to hold back. Patience is needed. The gift of food comes in its own time and for this we must wait.

THE JUDGEMENT

Waiting means holding back, not giving up or abandoning. You should still hold the inner certainty of reaching your goal. The Wise Leader has the courage to face reality without illusion or self-deception and avoid impatience and haste. This certainty and courage is the light that will shine upon the best path to take when the time comes.

THE IMAGE

The Wise Leader accepts that rain will follow the rising of the clouds. This is a destiny which should not be interfered with. Fortify yourself with good cheer and when fate comes, you will be ready.

5. WAITING

CHANGES

1. Although it is not yet close, there is an impending sense of danger. Do not waste any energy yet. Keep calm, and continue to tread a straight path.

2. The danger is drawing closer. Unrest can ensue if people start to panic and blame each other. Keep calm. Do not feed the danger with your own anger.

3. The danger has arrived. You have become entangled with it by not gathering enough strength to tackle it beforehand. Only by being cautious can you now avoid injury.

4. The danger is now of the utmost gravity. All you can do is stand fast, avoid aggravating the trouble and let destiny take its course.

5. Even in the midst of danger, periods of peace can ensue. Fortify yourself before the next struggle. Enjoy the moment without being deflected from the goal.

6. You have fallen into the pit and must yield. Even so, an outside intervention will bring rescue if you have the alertness to recognise it - and the deference to use it.

6. CONFLICT

Above: The Creative (Heaven)
Below: The Abysmal (Water)

THE CONDITION

Conflict is represented by: 1.The Creative's tendency to rise, and The Abysmal's (water's) tendency to flow down. 2. The Trigrams' attributes are danger and strength; force with cunning. 3. Inner cunning and outward determination indicate a quarrelsome person.

THE JUDGEMENT

Conflict can develop when you feel that you are in the right, but you encounter opposition. The Wise Leader is clear headed, and strong, yet willing to meet their opponent half-way. Do not let it continue too long as enmity will ensue. It takes a strong person to end it amicably. When conflict is within beware - it decreases the power to conquer danger without.

THE IMAGE

When opposing tendencies appear, conflict is inevitable. It can be avoided by ensuring that everyone is aware of their roles and duties, or that there is harmony between people to begin with.

6. CONFLICT

CHANGES

1. In the first stages of conflict it is better to drop the issue, especially if your opponent is stronger.

2. If your opponent has superior strength, retreat is not a disgrace and can prevent disaster. A wise approach is to be conciliatory . It will benefit everyone.

3. Do not lose the strength of your own nature. If you serve someone, do not seek work to achieve personal prestige. That way will conflict arise. Let the honour go to another. This is an ancient virtue.

4. If you are in conflict with a weaker opponent, and your success through their defeat will trouble your conscience, you will find a more profound peace if you turn back

5. If you are in the right, then seek out a good, powerful and just arbiter to resolve the conflict. You will win if you are right.

6. So you have carried the conflict through and triumphed. There is no lasting joy in it. Winning through conflict does not command respect. Conflict will not end. What is gained by force will be lost by force.

7. THE ARMY

Above: The Receptive (Earth)
Below: The Abysmal (Water)

THE CONDITION

This Hexagram represents water stored within the earth, like military power is stored up within a population. The power is invisible in peacetime, but ready to be called upon in times of war. All armies can be dangerous without discipline and obedience.

THE JUDGEMENT

The army needs discipline but it cannot be achieved by force. People's hearts and minds need to be captured and their enthusiasm awakened. It takes a strong leader to achieve this. If heading for war, the reasons for it and its aims need to be justified and explained clearly. The leader must also ensure that passion does not degenerate into acts of atrocity.

THE IMAGE

If you govern people humanely, and improve their economic situation, you will have the economic power to win respect militarily and the people's devotion and willingness to fight for you.

7. THE ARMY

CHANGES

1. At the start of a military action, order is essential. You must have a valid reason for action, and your troops must be organised. The onset of war is not a time for levity.

2. If there is a leader who is in touch with his army, sharing good and bad with them, he should be decorated and rewarded - to honour the whole army, not just him.

3. When there is interference with the proper chain of command or when the leader's power is usurped by others, there is only defeat to be gained.

4. If the leader is faced with a stronger enemy, an orderly retreat is the correct procedure. It is not a sign of courage to lead an army to its destruction.

5. The army needs an experienced leader when the enemy is engaged. Combat must not degenerate into a wild melèe. The rules of engagement need to be enforced.

6. When victory is achieved, reward the faithful with power and position. But beware of giving power to those who may later abuse it - reward them in other ways.

8. HOLDING TOGETHER

Above: The Abysmal (Water)
Below: The Receptive (Earth)

THE CONDITION

This hexagram represents union and mutual help. At the centre of the union is a leader of strong will. The leader is able to hold the people together by helping each individual see and feel the benefits of remaining keeping together as a group or community.

THE JUDGEMENT

Being the leader of a group holds great responsibility. It requires strength and consistency. Be sure that you are equal to the undertaking or there will be confusion and failure. It requires perseverance. If you have a real rallying point, people will come, and successful relationships will follow. If it is not the role for you, join in and be a follower.

THE IMAGE

The waters on the earth flow together and join when they can. Humans are subject to the same laws. A community of interests allows each to feel a part of the whole.

8. HOLDING TOGETHER

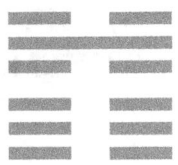

CHANGES

1. Sincerity is the basis for good relationships within a community. Not through fine words, but by inner strength that attracts good fortune to itself.

2. Respond to requests from above in the proper way and you will not lose yourself. Do not seek to gain the favours of those in a higher position or you will lose your dignity.

3. When among people from other backgrounds beware of being drawn into false intimacy. Be sociable, but be ready to re-join your own kind later.

4. Your relations with the centre of the community are established. You may safely show your loyalty and attachment openly.

5. The leader accepts those who join the group voluntarily, and also respects those who wish to go their own way. A good leader does not gain followers by flattery or coercion. They come of their own accord.

6. Pledge yourself to join and uphold the aims of the community. If you hesitate for too long the moment will be missed and misfortune will follow.

9. THE TAMING POWER OF THE SMALL

Above: The Gentle (Wind)
Below: The Creative (Heaven)

THE CONDITION

This Hexagram represents gentle winds bringing cloud, but without the strength to make rain. It is like a subordinate who gently restrains a domineering ruler. In times, when the strong are held in check by the weak, only through gentleness will the outcome be successful.

THE JUDGEMENT

This is a time to use gentle persuasion. Although there are obstacles still in the way, the situation is favourable with the prospect of ultimate success if you refrain from sweeping measures. You may be able to apply your influence in a way that restrains and subdues. This is a time for inner strength and outer gentleness. Be flexible in your approach.

THE IMAGE

The small wind can blow clouds, but without solidity it cannot produce lasting effects. If you cannot produce a great effect now, seek to refine the outward aspect of your nature in small ways.

9. THE TAMING POWER OF THE SMALL

CHANGES

1. If you are encountering obstructions, return to the way suited to your situation where you are free to advance or retreat. Do not apply force.

2. Although you want to press forward, the way is blocked. Do not advance and endanger yourself needlessly. Retreat without struggle and join others with like mind.

3. You attempt a forceful advance thinking that the obstruction is weak. Fate hinders the advance. Here the power lies with the weak. An offensive is doomed to failure.

4. You are a counsellor to a powerful person, which can be dangerous, especially as this person needs restraining. Use the power of sincerity and truth to achieve success.

5. In firm relationships each party complements the other. There is mutual and shared wealth. In this way you are rich indeed.

6. When success is near, be cautious. The culmination of small actions has worked, but do not parade your success. Be content with what you have achieved, lest you lose it.

10. TREADING

Above: The Creative (Heaven)
Below: The Joyous (Lake)

THE CONDITION

This Hexagram represents conduct, the right way of doing things. It is about the difference between high and low moral and social behaviour. The weak follows and treads upon the strong, but the strong takes it in good heart because there is compatibility between the two.

THE JUDGEMENT

When the weak person treads upon the strong it is as if they are trying to step on the tail of a tiger and not get bitten. And indeed the contact is in good humour so the strong does not harm the weak. The tiger does not bite. If you are dealing with wild or irritating people this is the time to behave with decorum. Remain calm and well-mannered.

THE IMAGE

Heaven (the Creative) and the Lake (The Joyous) show that people can be of different status . If the differences are unjust, there will be struggle. If they are accepted, there will be harmony.

10. TREADING

CHANGES

1. By simple conduct you can quietly follow your way. Be content with simplicity to make progress. By being too ambitious you risk becoming arrogant and spoilt.

2. By simple conduct and withdrawing from the bustle your path will be level. Seek nothing and ask for nothing and you will remain free of entanglements.

3. Inner weakness is combined with pressing ambition. The weak person, believing themselves to be strong invites disaster through recklessness.

4. When inner strength is combined with outer caution even dangerous enterprises succeed.

5. Be resolute in your conduct but remain aware of the dangers. Only in maintaining your awareness will success follow. Be strong, moderate and correct.

6. Review your conduct and judge yourself by the effects of your actions. It is only by the consequences of our action that we can judge what fortune will have in store for us. We are the fruits of our labours.

11. PEACE

Above: The Receptive (Earth)
Below: The Creative (Heaven)

THE CONDITION

This Hexagram represents Heaven placing itself beneath Earth. United, there is harmony, and like in springtime, there is growth and prospering. Calm prevails in the world and all people are content with their situations. It is a time for union and good relationships.

THE JUDGEMENT

When goodness and harmony are in control, things that were bad are changed for the better. It is as if you are imbued with the sprit of spring. You are under its spell and it is good. As spring is the season of the year for growth, so it is for you and those around you. Strength is within and yielding is without. It is a time of favour and success.

THE IMAGE

Heaven and Earth divide into seasons. Knowing these divisions, the Wise Leader is able to harness them for the good of others and herself. She can adjust to act in harmony with the season.

11. PEACE

CHANGES

1. Now is a time of prosperity. Now is a time to set out to accomplish something. Your influence will be wide, and others will support you.

2. There may still be hidden barriers to your undertaking. To overcome them you will need four things: forbearance of others; resoluteness in danger; vigilance of what lies ahead; impartiality to avoid divisiveness.

3. Enjoy your good fortune, but be aware that it cannot last. Keep mindful of danger and beware of the illusions of good fortune.

4. This is a time of harmony between those of higher and lower rank. It is the simplicity of mutual respect, and it comes naturally without being forced.

5. This is a time for people of the highest rank to submit themselves to the will of those of lower social standing. In such modesty is the great union of high and low.

6. You have had a time of great success, but now that time is ending. Do not resist, it will only make things worse. Withdraw into your intimate circle and keep your silence.

12. STANDSTILL

Above: The Creative (Heaven)
Below: The Receptive (Earth)

THE CONDITION

This Hexagram represents Heaven moving away from Earth as Earth sinks further into the depths. There is no harmony. There is standstill and decline. Summer has passed and the decay and stagnation of autumn is setting in.

THE JUDGEMENT

Somewhere along the path a wrong course has been taken. He actions of man have caused disharmony and confusion. The dark is within, the light is without. Inferior people are rising, better people are in decline. The Wise Leaders however are not diverted from their principles. They remain faithful to their beliefs and if no influence can be exerted, they withdraw.

THE IMAGE

In these times fruitful activity is impossible because the foundations are wrong. The Wise Leader is not tempted by offers of reward and wealth given by the weak. In this way danger is avoided.

12. STANDSTILL

CHANGES

1. If it is impossible to make your influence felt, withdraw. You will have succeeded in the higher sense of saving your inner self.

2. Do not mingle with inferior people, they are looking for a quick remedy. Stay calm and aloof. By preserving the fundamental principles you will suffer, but also show the true way to success.

3. When the people who have usurped high positions realise their weakness they will feel shame in their hearts although they may not show it. Better things are coming.

4. The time of standstill is about to change. Someone is needed with strength and authority, and the calling, to lead the way out. People will follow despite setbacks.

5. The right person to lead people out of the standstill is close by. This is a time of transition, and fear. Great caution is still needed. Nothing is secure yet.

6. It will take effort to bring standstill to and end. Peace can end of its own accord, but stagnation cannot change without man's creative effort.

13. FELLOWSHIP

Above: The Creative (Heaven)
Below: TheClinging (Fire)

THE CONDITION

This hexagram represents the peaceful union of strong people that needs one person of a yielding nature (the single yin line) to keep them together. Within the Fellowship there is light that shines from the inside, whilst strength is apparent on the outside.

THE JUDGEMENT

True fellowship requires all people to put needs of each other before the needs of the individual and for all to have a common and uplifting goal. A leader is needed to bring about this kind of fellowship. The leader must have clear and inspiring aims and the strength to carry them out. When unity prevails, great and dangerous tasks can be achieved.

THE IMAGE

To achieve fellowship there must be organisation with the diversity of people taken into account. It is not just the gathering together of a group. There must also be strength and clarity of purpose.

13. FELLOWSHIP

CHANGES

1. At the start, the union of people should take place out in the open. Ensure all have equality of access. Avoid actions of self-interest or secret arrangements.

2. Beware of factions and cliques forming. Low motives that welcome some but exclude others will lead to failure and humiliation.

3. There is a danger of secret plots hatching. The fellowship is in danger. People suspect each other of evils that they themselves are exhibiting. There is mistrust and people are becoming alienated.

4. Confrontation has occurred and the air has been cleared. Obstacles remain but the quarrel has brought people to their senses and they have returned to the right path.

5. Now that the struggle has been endured and worked through, the meeting of hearts can take place. People bound in fellowship weep together then laugh together.

6. If you have only joined in the fellowship of neighbours and not achieved universal brotherhood, there is no blame if you have done so for the benefit of the community.

14. POSESSION IN GREAT MEASURE

Above: The Clinging (Fire)
Below: The Creative (Heaven)

THE CONDITION

This hexagram represents a mild ruler who is surrounded by strong and able helpers. It relates to a person in authority who has inner strength but also modesty and kindness. The Great Possession is inside and it leads to heavenly treasure as well as earthly wealth.

THE JUDGEMENT

The yielding leader can hold and possess the strong through their virtue and unselfishness. The inner strength must be used to make correct decisions and to organise the helpers and provide them with clarity of purpose. The clarity comes from the leader knowing what is needed. The leader who is modest and kind brings culture and enlightenment.

THE IMAGE

The sun shines upon all things on the earth, be they good or evil. The Wise Leader combats the evil and promotes the good. In this way is the will of heaven fulfilled.

14. POSESSION IN GREAT MEASURE
CHANGES

1. Stay inwardly free of arrogance. You have yet to be tested by the difficulties to come so keep mindful of them. Keep away from what is harmful.

2. Keep your possessions and your talents mobile. Use them with flexibility in your tasks. Share responsibilities with others who can support you.

3. Place your possessions at the disposal of others if it will do good. Great goods can never endure as private property. A weak man is made weaker by great wealth.

4. Do not rely upon your wealth if you are rich. Do not envy the wealth of others if you are poor. If you possess everything as if you possess nothing you are rich indeed.

5. Use your internal and external wealth with dignity, not as a means of buying people. Be sincere and unaffected and people will be confident in you.

6. At the height of power and wealth, success will only come to the modest. The devoted and the true are blessed. There is nothing that does not further them.

15. MODESTY

Above: The Receptive (Earth)
Below: Keeping still (Mountain)

THE CONDITION

This Hexagram represents the lofty mountain being placed beneath the lowly earth. The function of Modesty is to raise the lowly person. The function of Modesty for the highly placed person is to provide them with a heavenly light. They shine with the light of wisdom

THE JUDGEMENT

Modesty lies in honouring others and not boasting about personal achievements. It is the way of heaven to fill what is empty and empty what is full. If the Wise Leader is empty of arrogance and pride, they shall be filled with greatness. The way to expansion is via contraction, this is the immutable law. Modesty wins love. Arrogance brings destruction.

THE IMAGE

There is inner wealth. Within the earth is a mountain. Reduce what is too much, increase what is too little. Work towards equity. Modify the extremes that cause discontent.

15. MODESTY

CHANGES

1. Be modest about your modesty and difficult things can be achieved. Attend to tasks directly and simply. Be unassuming and you will avoid resistance.

2. Your outward behaviour expresses your inner self. Favour will come to those whose words and deeds are congruent. In such ways can you influence without effort.

3. Through modesty can you gain support and strength to push things through to the end. If you allow yourself to be dazzled by the prospect of fame, difficulties will arise.

4. Avoiding your responsibilities is not true modesty. True modesty requires unassuming action not inertia. Show interest in the tasks you carry out and keep things moving.

5. Do not confuse modesty with weakness. Take strong action if you have to, but do it in a way that is not offensive, and is not done to raise your own profile with others.

6. In difficult times the weak person will for others to blame. The truly modest person will seek to rectify their own weaknesses first through self discipline.

16. ENTHUSIASM

Above: The Arousing (Thunder)
Below: The Receptive (Earth)

THE CONDITION

The Trigrams represent devotion within and movement without. Devotion with movement is enthusiasm. The movement should be along the line of least resistance. Thus will it be in accord with natural events and human life. The enthusiasm engendered can carry all before it.

THE JUDGEMENT

To arouse enthusiasm the Wise Leader acts in accord with the spirit of the people and the movement of natural things. Act with people in accord with laws that are deeply rooted in popular sentiment. Violating this sentiment can lead to resentment. Enthusiasm enables helpers to be found who can support the achievement of great things.

THE IMAGE

As summer begins there is thunder and rain to refresh all things and resolve tension. There are ceremonies, both solemn and with song and dance, to bring joy and relief.

16. ENTHUSIASM

CHANGES

1. Maintain your caution and reserve. Do not get enthusiastic about your own advancement or high connections. Be enthusiastic for that which unifies yourself with others.

2. Beware of being misled by illusions. Flatter not those above, nor neglect those below. If there are signs of discord, withdraw into self reliance.

3. Maintain your self reliance. Do not become dependent on any one figure or leader. Beware too of hesitation. You must seize the right moment if you are to succeed.

4. When you are free of hesitation and sure in your task, you will attract willing and enthusiastic followers. You will keep their support by your support of them.

5. There may be frustration that your enthusiasm is obstructed. Keep to your task, such pressure can actually help, it provides a focus for action.

6. It is not good if your enthusiasm is a delusion. Yet, all is not lost if you realise this. In any case it never lasts. Awakening from a false enthusiasm is good.

17. FOLLOWING

Above: The Joyous (Lake)
Below: The Arousing (Thunder)

THE CONDITION

The Trigram's attributes unite movement with joyousness. People will join a movement that is filled with joy. The strong person defers to the weak and shows consideration to them. In this way the weak are moved to follow the strong.

THE JUDGEMENT

If you are a leader you must know how to adapt. Before you rule you must learn to serve. Followers cannot be secured by force or guile. This will only attract resistance. Be sure that your aims are honourable, and be aware that even joyous movement can lead to evil consequences. If you are to follow, ensure too that the person you will follow is doing right.

THE IMAGE

In winter thunder is at rest. The Wise Leader too takes rest and looks inward. Whatever the time or season, the Wise Leader adapts to it. This is the way to obtain a following. Look to the laws of nature.

17. FOLLOWING

CHANGES

1. Be responsive to the views of others. Do not only listen to those who hold the same opinions as you. Mingle and meet with people with as wide a range of views as possible.

2. If you mix with unworthy people, you may lose your connections with the good, trustworthy people and lose the good within yourself. Take care choosing your friends.

3. Connections with good people will allow you to lose the inferior and superficial. Keep aware of what you want and do not be distracted by passing whims

4. You may have flatterers around you seeking personal advantage. Do not get drawn by them. Be free of ego and clear in purpose and you will see through them.

5. Everyone needs a guiding light. If you have one, follow it with sincerity and conviction and good fortune will prevail.

6. The Wise Leader who has put the turmoil of the world behind her, comes back into the world to help a someone of high standing. There is great honour in such an invitation.

18. REMOVING DECAY

Above: Keeping still (Mountain)
Below: The Gentle (Wind)

THE CONDITION

This Hexagram represents a bowl within which worms are breeding. It is about inner corruption and decay. There has been corruption, things have been spoiled. At some time there has been an abuse of human freedom. This needs to be rectified. The decay needs to be removed.

THE JUDGEMENT

Inertia and indifference have led to the decay. The to be replaced by energy and decisiveness. The causes of the decay need to be identified, so be cautious before you start to take action. The way of action needs to be safe, so be cautious when you start. New beginnings follow old endings. Act to remove the decay and such an undertaking will be favoured.

THE IMAGE

The Wise Leader devotes energy to removing the decay of debased attitudes and behaviour. Like the wind, he stirs what is stagnant, and then provides tranquility and nourishment like the mountain.

18. REMOVING DECAY

CHANGES

1. Decay has come from the too rigid approach of others As you work on the remedy, do not blame them. It is not yet deep rooted but still tread carefully.

2. In acting, keep to the middle way. Be gentle on the inner weakness of others and avoid action that is too drastic or could hurt.

3. Not everything will go smoothly when you work on removing decay. This must be expected. You may feel slight remorse but your good intentions will compensate for minor mistakes.

4. If decay is beginning to show, do not let it fester or grow. If it continues unchecked humiliation will follow. You will gain nothing by letting it drift.

5. You cannot deal with the decay alone. You need able helpers. Work with them to change what needs to be changed with energy and forbearance and you will succeed.

6. The Wise Leader may be justified in not involving herself in the reforming activities of others. She may have the higher aims of working for the good of all mankind.

19. APPROACH

Above: The Receptive (Earth)
Below: The Joyous (Lake)

THE CONDITION

This Hexagram is about 'Becoming Great'. It represents the time after the winter solstice, when light begins to ascend again. There is a need for the person in authority to consider their approach towards other people both during and after their rise to power.

THE JUDGEMENT

Spring is coming and it is a time for high and low to work closely together with determination and make the most of the propitious time. Spring does not last forever and the light-giving aspects will be reversed. Remain aware and look out for signs of impending evil and deal with it before it becomes a reality.

THE IMAGE

The Wise Leader is like a deep, inexhaustible lake in her readiness to teach, and as wide and boundless as the earth in her tolerance and care for others, no matter who they may be.

19. APPROACH

CHANGES

1. As you rise towards greatness be steadfast in your pursuit of what is right. O not let yourself be carried away by the current of the time.

2. A call may come from above. Have the inner strength and will to respond quickly and with awareness that a descent follows a rise.

3. Beware of complacency when things are going well. Likewise beware of relaxing too much and becoming careless. The Wise Leader will catch himself in this, and rectify it.

4. When you have reached a great height, draw those of equal ability into your circle regardless of their background or social standing. Greater success will follow.

5. Be wise in the choice of your helpers. Allow them a free hand. Do not interfere and dilute their expertise. Maintain your self-restraint.

6. The Wise Leader who has withdrawn from the world may decide to return and assist in the undertakings of others. This will bring blessings to those she teaches and helps.

20. CONTEMPLATION

Above: The Gentle (Wind)
Below: The Receptive (Earth)

THE CONDITION

The hexagram reminds us of a tower, something that you can look out from, and also something that can be seen from a great distance. In human terms it represents someone who can see things via contemplation, yet someone who is also highly visible and sets a lofty example.

THE JUDGEMENT

By contemplating on the spiritual side of life and its meaning, the Wise Leader can develop faith and understanding of the great mysteries. The expression of the natural laws becomes a way of being. Inner concentration leads to spiritual contemplation. From this comes trust and devotion from others. This will happen of its own accord, naturally.

THE IMAGE

The person with high standing goes everywhere, like the wind. He is receptive the true sentiments of people and is not deceived. This affects people, and they are swayed, like grass in the wind.

20. CONTEMPLATION

CHANGES

1. A simple view of your situation may not be sufficient. It is wise to contemplate more deeply. Consider all of the prevailing forces. Do not be superficial in your thinking.

2. Beware of contemplating on yourself only. Put yourself in the shoes of others involved and try to understand their motives.

3. By contemplative reflection you can objectively see the effects of your actions. Realising the effect you are having enables an accurate judgement of how to proceed.

4. When someone knows the secrets of the way that things can flourish, they should be given the authority and independence to act and achieve.

5. No matter how high your standing, self examination is crucial. Examine the results of your labours. When the results are good, and your inner motivations are good, you can be satisfied.

6. The Wise Leader, liberated from ego, contemplates the laws of life rather than self or effects. This is where peace resides.

21. BITING THROUGH

Above: The Clinging (Fire)
Below: The Arousing (Thunder)

THE CONDITION

This Hexagram represents an obstruction within an open mouth. The removal of the obstruction requires a firm bite. If someone is causing disruption or difficulties, the force of the law needs to be implemented, and an appropriate penalties may need to be meted out.

THE JUDGEMENT

Someone or something is blocking the way and the blockage needs to be removed. It will not go away on its own. Action needs to be taken. However, the action needs to be carefully balanced between harshness and gentleness. Not too much nor too little of either. Use gentleness to prevent cruelty and it will not be a weakness. Yet act firmly and maintain respect.

THE IMAGE

Apply mild and severe penalties to fit the nature of the misdeeds. Use thunder and lightening: clarity and fear. Make clear what the penalties for misdemeanours will be, and enforce them.

21. BITING THROUGH

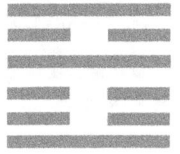

CHANGES

1. At the first wrongdoing, be light in your punishment. Use it as a warning. Thus do you avoid blame and keep respect.

2. Your anger may be aroused and it may block out your common sense for a short time. Perhaps you act too harshly. But if you are dealing with a hardened opponent, this is understandable.

3. Either you are not letting go of old issues, or you are not showing the kind of authority that you need to. Let bygones be bygones, or take swift and definite action.

4. The opponents are powerful, and they need some form of penalty or punishment. It will be difficult but you need to be steadfast. Be hard and straight in your action. Like an arrow.

5. The situation is not an easy one. You need to be true and impartial. Keep to the middle way and avoid extremes. Be aware of the possible dangers.

6. If someone places themselves above the law, and heeds not the judgements or warning against them, misfortune will follow.

22. GRACE

Above: Keeping still (Mountain)
Below: The Clinging (Fire)

THE CONDITION

This hexagram represents fire breaking out from the depths of the earth. It rises up to illuminate and beautify the mountain. In human terms it represents adornment, grace and beauty of form. It is pleasing and ordered, not chaotic.

THE JUDGEMENT

Gracefulness and adornment are not essential, but they are pleasing and as such are best used sparingly and in unpretentious ways. As long as there is strength within, a little adornment will do no harm. Grace and beauty can shine forth most strikingly from an inner clarity. Without this, it is superficial and meaningless.

THE IMAGE

There is clarity within and quiet without. Tranquility can come when desire is silenced. Set aside some time for meditation, even if only briefly.

22. GRACE

CHANGES

1. Take responsibility for yourself and your growth and advancement. It is more graceful to walk than take a ride on the back of someone else's labours.

2. Beware of superficial adornments. What is on the inside is more important than external appearances. Beware of vanity.

3. Beware of being drawn in to the feeling of indolence and laziness that grace and adornment can bring. Do not preen yourself. There is work to do. Charm and beauty can quickly disappear.

4. If you begin to question whether all the external glitter and adornments are better than simplicity. Your doubt is the answer. Simple friendships and relationships are greater than the adornments of success.

5. Sincerity is what counts now. You may not have much to offer in material terms, but being true will gain respect and love.

6. To achieve true grace, there is no need to hide what is inside with any kind of external ornamentation at all. Just allow your inner beauty to shine forth.

23. SPLITTING APART

Above: Keeping still (Mountain)
Below: The Receptive (Earth)

THE CONDITION

This Hexagram represents a house splitting apart. Only the roof remains intact. The building has been undermined from below. There has been a strong disintegrating influence that has been exerted over a long period, slowly and imperceptibly. Total collapse is imminent.

THE JUDGEMENT

This is a bad time. The best course of action to take is to take no action. Sitting it out will accord with the two Trigrams' attributes of inner docility and outward stillness. The bleakness of the current circumstances are due to time. But it will pass, like a season. In this time it is wisdom, not cowardice, to submit to the inevitable and do nothing.

THE IMAGE

A mountain that does not have a broad base is more likely to topple in adverse conditions. For people, a broad base is developed through benevolence, like the earth that carries all.

23. SPLITTING APART

CHANGES

1. There could be movement afoot to undermine your position or turn your friends against you. But do nothing yet. Just wait.

2. You are becoming isolated and without help from any side. Be very cautious. Avoid taking too firm a stance. Do not be stubborn, it will lead to failure.

3. You are surrounded by adversity and the mistrust of others. Avoid listening to those around you who may be false, even if you are seen as being in opposition to them.

4. Misfortune is at hand. It has reached its peak and cannot be avoided. All you can do it wait and endure. It will pass eventually.

5. The misfortune is reaching its end (the strong Yang line at the top). The negative will become influenced by the positive and start to change. Those who may have been plotting, will now listen to reason.

6. Better times are returning, like seeds that grow from fallen fruit. Evil feeds on good, and also on itself. With the strength to do nothing, you let evil consume itself.

24. RETURN

Above: The Receptive (Earth)
Below: The Arousing (Thunder)

THE CONDITION

This Hexagram represents a turning point. A strong Yang line enters from below. It is the return of the light. The time of darkness and decay has passed. This turning point is not forced but natural. It happens like the change of the seasons. It is in accord with the time.

THE JUDGEMENT

The transformation from darkness to light is easy because it is a natural occurrence. The old can be discarded and the new embraced. The meeting of friends is well favoured. It is a time for sharing. Now is also the time to turn away from external confusion and cultivate the inner light. But beware of taking action prematurely. The tide is only just turning.

THE IMAGE

Movement, the Arousing, is just beginning. The Wise Leader takes rest and rebuilds their their strength. Just as health returns after illness, tenderness and care is needed to help recuperate.

24. RETURN

CHANGES

1. If you are thinking of taking a course of action that does not feel quite right. Stop now. If you continue to force the issue, no good will come of it.

2. Take guidance from a good friend. Any decision of what to do must be your own, but the advice or thoughts of someone with wisdom will help you make it.

3. The time for change is recognised, which is good. However, beware of beginning to change but then going back, and then changing again. There is danger in doing this.

4. There are others around you who persist in the wrong ways of the past. Do not remain on their path. You know the right way now. Stay with it.

5. Avoid looking for excuses not to change. If you have done wrong before, acknowledge this with dignity. Choosing good now will bring rewards.

6. Do not miss the turning point by obstinately continuing your current path. Change needs to take place, otherwise there will great misfortune.

25. INNOCENCE

Above: The Creative (Heaven)
Below: The Arousing (Thunder)

THE CONDITION

This Hexagram represents the innocence that is achieved when ulterior motives, cunning and plotting are discarded. Thus is the inner self in accord with the will of heaven. There is no conscious purpose, no selfishness. It is about living in the here and now.

THE JUDGEMENT

Allow your instinct to judge what is right. Think not of ulterior reward or personal advantage, for this would bring misfortune. Resist any pressure to take action that you know is wrong and would bring shame. Use your instinct, in innocence, to do what is right. Place trust in your own feelings. If they are virtuous, success will follow.

THE IMAGE

Thunder rolls under heaven. There is movement, like in Spring, when new life begins to grow in the primal innocence of its original state. The Wise Leader uses this new life to foster and care for all people.

25. INNOCENCE

CHANGES

1. Follow your heart with confidence. The original impulses of it are always good, following them will bring good fortune and the achievement of your aims.

2. Take each separate task as it comes. Do not look too far ahead to the future. Complete each task well, and a successful end result will follow naturally.

3. You cannot trust everybody. Sometimes people will let you down. This is the way of things and you must accommodate it without letting it steer you away from your course.

4. What is good inside you can be covered up, but not destroyed. Do not be anxious if another is trying to lead you away from your path. Your inner light will shine through.

5. An unexpected evil may arrive from without like an illness. If has not come from within, take no action or medicine and it will disappear. Let nature take its course.

6. If the time is not right for further action, wait quietly. Pushing now will be in opposition to fate and you will not succeed.

26. THE TAMING POWER OF THE GREAT

Above: Keeping still (Mountain)
Below: The Creative (Heaven)

THE CONDITION

This Hexagram represents the concept of holding firm and Keeping still. There is great power within, but outer stillness. The concept is of holding firm by: holding together, holding back, and holding close those who can support you and acknowledging their value to you.

THE JUDGEMENT

This is a time to consider all the creative powers and other resources you have gained in life. Keep still and reflect on these daily and your strength will grow. By such inner acknowledgement of your own strengths and qualities, you will be able to act correctly and with vigour, and undertake great things when the time comes.

THE IMAGE

The strength of Heaven lies within the stillness of the Mountain. There are hidden riches. The Wise Leader considers the great words of history, and applies them to give the past a current reality.

26. THE TAMING POWER OF THE GREAT

CHANGES

1. Danger is at hand. Do not force your way forward. You have energy and resources stored and ready. Wait for a better opportunity to to release them.

2. A danger has presented itself. Do not struggle against it. It is superior. Be content to wait. You still have the resources to take vigorous action later.

3. A way forward has opened. Take it, but keep your goal in mind. Taking a friend with you will help. There is still danger. Be careful, and beware of sudden attacks.

4. Think ahead. The horns of a young bull can be removed before they grow and become dangerous. Taking such preventative action will bring success.

5. The way to deal with the danger that confronts you is to deal with the root causes of it. The tusk of the wild boar is not dangerous if the boar has been tamed.

6. When the danger has passed and the obstruction overcome, the energy and resources you have accumulated will take you forward easily to success.

27. PROVIDING NOURISHMENT

Above: Keeping still (Mountain)
Below: The Arousing (Thunder)

THE CONDITION

This Hexagram depicts an open mouth and an upward moving lower jaw and therefore represents the giving and receiving of nourishment. Nourishment is related to the care of oneself and other people in a spiritual or emotional sense.

THE JUDGEMENT

The nourishment and support you provide to yourself or to others must be healthy and wholesome. Cultivate the higher parts of your own and others' nature, not the baser instincts. Choose carefully those to whom you will provide nourishment. Choose those who will respond positively and who may provide nourishment to others in turn.

THE IMAGE

Thunder stirs from within the still Mountain. The Wise Leader chooses words with care. She is tranquil in her actions and temperate in her eating and drinking. Avoiding extremes cultivates character.

27. PROVIDING NOURISHMENT

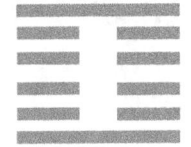

CHANGES

1. Do not look with envy or discontent upon people in better circumstances. This will not bring respect. Hold on to your self-reliance.

2. Beware of seeking support from others when you do not really need it. Stand on your own two feet. If you are capable of looking after yourself, do so or the respect of others may be lost.

3. Nourishment is different than gratification, which is desire. No good can come from the pursuit of pleasure alone.

4. If you work for the good of all, no blame can come from actively seeking the help of others.

5. If the way forward is too great a struggle, seek out someone who has the wisdom to help you. Do not take on too much. Be aware of your own limitations

6. If a wise friend brings nourishment, it should be accepted. If they aware of the dangers, and still accept the great responsibility of helping, blessings will come to all.

28. GREAT HEAVINESS

Above: The Abysmal (Water)
Below: The Abysmal (Water)

THE CONDITION

This Hexagram is depicted by four strong lines in the centre and two weak lines on the outside. It represents a carrying pole which is sagging because of the weight of the load. It is close to breaking. The condition must pass or be changed. There will be misfortune otherwise.

THE JUDGEMENT

Action has been taken that has gone too far. It is an exceptional time, and exceptional measures need to be taken. But force is not the answer. First, the causes of the situation need to be examined, and then action to move into a different situation can take place more safely. The transition phase requires great inner strength. This is a momentous time.

THE IMAGE

The lake has risen into a flood. The time is exceptional, but transitory. The Wise Leader stands alone, deeply rooted as a tree which can endure, and remains undaunted.

28. GREAT HEAVINESS

CHANGES

1. The time is extraordinary, so extraordinary caution needs to be taken. Any action needs to be planned with careful attention to detail.

2. New aspect of the situation may grow quickly. Joining with others who you may not usually mix with can shed new light, and possibly point to a new way forward.

3. Obstinacy in pushing ahead despite advice to the contrary can bring catastrophe. If lose the support of others, your burden will weigh even more heavily.

4. Accepting the support and help of others will help to ease the burden. However, if you misuse their help for your own gain, you will lose out eventually.

5. Make sure that you ally yourself with the right people, otherwise you may waste energy. You need the support of the many, not the patronage of the few.

6. When the extraordinary situation reaches a climax, if you have done as much as you could with courage and good intention, there is no blame.

29. THE ABYSMAL

Above: Keeping still (Mountain)
Below: The Gentle (Wind)

THE CONDITION

This Hexagram represents plunging into danger. The light of the two Yang lines is enclosed by the darkness of the Yin lines. The light force is within, but the danger is without. It does not come from your own incorrect attitude, thus you can escape from it with correct behaviour

THE JUDGEMENT

When confronted with difficulties, be sincere and correct in your conduct. Be like the water that surrounds you - flow on and on, shrinking not from any deep plunge or fall, yet always true to your nature. Take action with thoroughness, go forward. Do not wait. The very threat of danger can be a prompt for protective action which can prevent misfortune.

THE IMAGE

The Wise Leader is like water: consistent and dependable. He holds firm to what is good within him and walks ever onward in lasting virtue. He does not get engulfed by desires or passions.

29. THE ABYSMAL

CHANGES

1. You have not shown the strength to avoid danger. It surrounds you to the extent that you are getting used to it. You are in danger of losing your way.

2. When surrounded by danger, remain calm. Be content if you manage simply to avoid being overcome by it. Moving forward in small ways is a good course of action.

3. Every step, forward or backward leads to danger. Escape is impossible. Like in a bog, struggling will only make you sink more quickly. Just wait until a way shows itself.

4. In times of danger just be yourself. What you have to offer may be simple and meagre, but if it is offered with sincerity it will be accepted.

5. Be content with what you have achieved. Further ambition will bring further dangers. Pushing for greater things will not succeed in these dangerous times.

6. You have lost the right way. Until you find it again you will be imprisoned by your inability to act correctly. Until you change there is no prospect of escape.

30. THE CLINGING

Above: The Clinging (Fire)
Below: The Clinging (Fire)

THE CONDITION

In this Hexagram, the dark lines (Yin) cling on to the light lines (Yang). It represents 'clinging to something' and 'brightness'. Like fire that has no definite form but clings to an object and burns brightly. The Clinging also relates to the radiance of nature, and a bright, clear mind

THE JUDGEMENT

On the outside there is strength, whilst on the inside there is the docility of a cow. When inner and outer clarity of purpose is achieved, brightness shines through and brings good fortune and spiritual transformation. Dependence on the natural way of things is the fuel that keeps the fire burning brightly. Cling to what is good and right.

THE IMAGE

The double Trigram represents the light that endures. The Wise Leader causes light to spread and illuminate all quarters of the world, and to shine ever more deeply into the nature of man.

30. THE CLINGING

CHANGES

1. It is dawn. At the start of the day be aware of the surrounding haste and bustle, but be calm within. Do not allow yourself to be swept along. Real concentration is needed.

2. The yellow light of midday brings good fortune. It is the light that symbolises high culture and art. Moderation and control is needed. Take the middle way.

3. At sunset, there is the reminder that all life is transitory. Keep to the cultivated path. Do not waste yourself with superficiality or lamenting the passage of time.

4. Beware of burning out your flame too quickly. A slow burning will bring more lasting results.

5. There is a weakness that causes tears and sadness. However, the path being taken is true and straight and will nevertheless lead to good fortune.

6. To attain maturity and wisdom, seek to find the causes of bad habits and eradicate them. Ensure you deal with the major issues, not the minor ones. 'Punish the leaders but spare the followers'.

31. INFLUENCE

Above: The Joyous (Lake)
Below: Keeping still (Mountain)

THE CONDITION

This Hexagram represents courtship and wooing. Strength and stillness within finds a joyous response from without. There is a mutual influencing, attraction and affinity between the male and the female principles. The masculine happily subordinates itself to the feminine.

THE JUDGEMENT

It is the stillness within that keeps joyousness in check, and prevents excess. Now is the time for the strong to defer to the weak and show consideration. It is time for courtship, not seduction. For a successful union to take place, there must be mutual attraction and influence. This includes influencing the hearts of others in order to achieve peace.

THE IMAGE

The Wise Leader attracts the hearts of others by being receptive. Like the lake at the top of the mountain, she has a humble and free mind. Not being full of herself, people seek her wisdom.

31. INFLUENCE

CHANGES

1. You are starting to have the inklings of plans for the future. They are not formalised yet so there is no external impact, good or bad.

2. Beware of being forced by others to take action. The right time to influence and act has yet to come. Wait until you are compelled to take action.

3. Beware of simply chasing your desires and avoid yielding to the whims of others. Listen to your own heart. This is the basis of freedom.

4. Don't try to manipulate or control others. This will cause nothing but stress and exhaustion., and they will not follow you. Only right-minded influencing will work.

5. Influence others with calmness and flexibility, not rigidity. If you cannot be influenced, how can you influence others? Influence what is outside by the quiet power you possess on the inside .

6. Do not attempt to influence people in a superficial way. People are not influenced by wagging tongues or empty speeches.

32. DURATION

Above: The Arousing (Thunder)
Below: Gentle (Wind)

THE CONDITION

This Hexagram represents the enduring union between the paired natural elements of Thunder and Wind. It represents the longevity of deep human relationships, like marriage or civil partnership. There is a strong, directing partner, and a gentle following partner, and the union is enduring.

THE JUDGEMENT

There is duration when things are not worn down by obstacles. This duration is natural and subject to the laws of heaven. It is not stagnant. There is movement like the breathing in and exhaling of air that keeps one alive. Keep whole, self contained and self renewing. Change with the times but keep your overall sense of direction.

THE IMAGE

Thunder and wind are mobile, the apparent opposite of duration, but it is the laws of nature that govern them that endure. So the Wise Leader is not rigid or immobile. Her inner law is firm and enduring.

32. DURATION

CHANGES

1. Lasting results cannot be achieved quickly. Do not demand to have everything at once. It must be worked for. Attempt to achieve all and you will achieve nothing.

2. Beware of overreaching yourself. What you seek to achieve may be beyond your strength. Control your inner desires and avoid misfortune.

3. Do not lose your inner consistency of character. Do not be at the mercy of superficial hopes and fears aroused by the outside world.

4. Be certain that you are seeking to achieve the right thing. Do not hunt where there is no game. Seek what you want in the right place and in the right way.

5. For some, doing the right thing requires adaptability. For others, lifelong dedication and constancy is the key to success. Be sure that your own approach is right for you.

6. Beware of being perpetually busy but achieving nothing. Restlessness prevents thoroughness and will not be in accord with natural law.

33. RETREAT

Above: The Creative (Heaven)
Below: Keeping still (Mountain)

THE CONDITION

This Hexagram represents darkness entering from below, as the light retreats. This form of withdrawal is natural, like the end of a season. This form of retreat is not the flight of the weak, but the calculated withdrawal of the wise, for it is not the time to fight.

THE JUDGEMENT

Success will come if you retreat correctly and at the right time. Avoid forcing a way forward in any great strides. This will not work. Strive only for small successes. You are not abandoning the field but seeking to fight small countermeasures. This will keep the enemy at bay until the most opportune time to withdraw altogether with all your power intact.

THE IMAGE

No matter how high the dark mountain is, heaven is always above it. So is the Wise Leader above the dealings of lesser people. There is no hatred, just dignified reserve which works to dissipate evil.

33. RETREAT

CHANGES

1. You are at the tail-end of a retreating army and the enemy is in pursuit. There is great danger. Remain still. Do not even consider taking action. This is the best way.

2. It may seem like good is retreating from evil, but You will reach your goal through perseverance and rightness of thought and deed. It is not weak to withdraw now.

3. Others are preventing you from retreating to a safe distance. It is frustrating and dangerous. Keep only people around you who are as determined to succeed as you are.

4. Be wise and aim for a willing and friendly withdrawal. The lesser person will not have the inner self-determination to succeed in this and should seek wiser guidance.

5. The wise person will recognise the moment to withdraw on good terms. When the decision is made, be resolute and not led astray by irrelevant considerations.

6. You have no doubts about what to do, so do it. Inner detachment is established. You are free to withdraw and you can accomplish it with cheerfulness and good grace.

34. THE POWER OF THE GREAT

Above: The Arousing (Thunder)
Below: The Creative (Heaven)

THE CONDITION

This Hexagram shows four strong and powerful Yang lines entering from below. They are about to ascend higher. There is great strength within and movement without. Strength and action. This is a time where the great are powerful. But power needs to used wisely.

THE JUDGEMENT

The power within you is surging onward and upward. It has gone beyond half way. You need to be certain that you are acting for the good. Beware of the debilitating effects of misusing your power. Having strength within and movement without means having the strength to remain focused in one's rightness of action. Without rightness there is no greatness.

THE IMAGE

Thunder moves in accordance with heaven. So to do the actions of the Wise Leader. True greatness requires acting in accordance with what is right and in harmony with the natural order of things.

34. THE POWER OF THE GREAT

CHANGES

1. Beware of acting too forcefully. Do not let the power you have go to your head. Using too much force will bring misfortune.

2. There is little resistance to your onward movement. As such, it is time to be wary of becoming over-confident. Keep your inner equilibrium. If you have true power, you will be able to do this and hold yourself back.

3. Do not boast about your power. This will only lead to hostility and fruitless entanglements (like a goat butting against a hedge). Used correctly, your power will be invisible.

4. Success will come through quite perseverance. The power that does not show externally can still move heavy loads (like the strength of a cart being in its axle).

5. You can afford to lose your goat-like stubbornness and aggression. You do not need them now. There are no major obstacles to overcome.

6. Like the goat butting the hedge, you have become entangled. There is stalemate. Stop struggling and compose yourself. Things will right themselves in time.

35. PROGRESS

Above: The Clinging (Fire)
Below: The Receptive (Earth)

THE CONDITION

This Hexagram represents the sun (fire) rising up and over the earth. It means rapid and easy progress. Progress can also mean growth, improvement and greater clarity of vision. The Hexagrams Upward(46) & Development (53) are also about progress, but this is the strongest.

THE JUDGEMENT

There is clarity above and devotion below. There is a good leader whom others follow willingly. Those in higher authority reward the good leader without jealousy. In such a situation great progress can be achieved. Helping another flourish will bring good fortune to all concerned. Those who serve others prosper and gain influence for themselves.

THE IMAGE

As the sun rises over the earth its light becomes clearer. It emerges through the dark early mists. So the Wise Leader seeks to achieve the clarity of vision that shines through the darkness.

35. PROGRESS

CHANGES

1. There is pressure to make progress but the way forward is unclear. Just continue to do what is right and a clearer direction will emerge.

2. Progress can be frustrated when seeking help that is not forthcoming. Persevere with the course of correct action. It will reap rewards.

3. When you have the backing and encouragement of others, progress will be made. Do not worry about losing your independence. There is no shame in accepting help.

4. To progress dishonourably to achieve wealth or prestige would be a grave mistake. Rats shun exposure. If you feel like hiding your actions from others, you are in danger.

5. Do not be concerned if you feel you have not taken advantage of every opportunity. The important thing is that you are still making progress.

6. Forceful progress can be dangerous. Misfortune will follow if you push too hard, and especially if you push other people too hard.

36. DARKENING OF THE LIGHT

Above: The Receptive (Earth)
Below: The Clinging (Fire)

THE CONDITION

The sun (fire) sinks below the earth. The light is veiled but not extinguished. This Hexagram symbolises a time where a darker force or person is in control and has a higher authority than the forces of good or wiser, better people.

THE JUDGEMENT

There is much adversity all around you. You must remain steadfast and not allow yourself to be swept along by the unfavourable circumstances. You can remain steadfast by maintaining your inner light whilst being outwardly yielding. Another way is to hide your light to everyone but yourself so that only you know that inside you are still good and virtuous.

THE IMAGE

The Wise Leader does not fall into the dark ways of others. She endures what is happening without awakening the anger of the evil forces that surround her. She keeps her inner light glowing.

36. DARKENING OF THE LIGHT

CHANGES

1. If you stay true to your principles you will go hungry rather than eat without honour.
Staying on the right path causes such deprivation. Even your friends may mistrust you.

2. You may be suffering, but by helping others in danger, you will help yourself. Good fortune will follow from placing others above yourself and doing your duty.

3. A major force of evil has been identified and stopped. There is a victory but beware of being too hasty reversing past misdeeds. Time is needed to readjust.

4. You find yourself close to the cause of the present dire situation. Move away. Staying close will do no good. Save yourself to fight another day.

5. If you cannot escape the danger you must be doubly cautious. Real firmness is needed. Hide your real sentiments and stay true to your innermost convictions despite the misery.

6. The darkness has reached its climax. Yet, when evil has consumed all good, it will consume itself and light will return.

37. THE FAMILY

Above: The Gentle (Wind)
Below: The Clinging (Fire)

THE CONDITION

This Hexagram represents wind created by fire. It relates to influence that spreads outwards from within. The family (traditional or modern) is a microcosm of society. The home is where duty is combined with natural affection. This approach can bring order everywhere.

THE JUDGEMENT

For a family to succeed, there are certain roles and responsibilities that need to be fulfilled by all the family or group members such as fathers, wives, sons and daughters, or their equivalents. There needs to be authority, loyalty, the desire to serve, moral strength, friendship and love. When the family is in order, so too will the society outside.

THE IMAGE

Wind comes forth from fire. Influence works like this as well. From inside to outside. The Wise Leader is aware of this and so takes care with her words and then acts consistently with them.

37. THE FAMILY

CHANGES

1. Each person, especially those younger, or with little experience must be made aware of what behaviour is appropriate, and what is not. Aim to achieve order at the outset.

2. There will be order if someone takes responsibility for social and spiritual pursuits. Someone with gentleness and perseverance will be best suited for this.

3. Allow people their freedom, but within well defined boundaries. Administer any discipline swiftly but only when it is needed and without undue severity.

4. Be aware that the financial situation of the family or group needs to be controlled well. Income and expenditure need to be properly balanced.

5. Like a good King, the leader of the family needs wisdom, and to nothing that invokes fear in others. Love should reign and be the means of achieving the desired ends.

6. The leader of the family or group must cultivate their inner clarity and goodness. The leader must take responsibility for everyone, and especially themselves.

38. OPPOSITION

Above: The Clinging (Fire)
Below: The Joyous (Lake)

THE CONDITION

By nature, fire and water are opposed. Water flows down, fire rises up. The movements are opposed. Thus this Hexagram represents misunderstanding, opposition and estrangement. There is disagreement between people. Viewpoints differ greatly.

THE JUDGEMENT

Do not proceed with force. This would only increase the opposition. Go forward in small steps only. The opposition may be seen as an obstruction, but if it part of a whole, a polarity, it can be the font of great things. Opposition highlights the need for a bridge. After opposition there can only be union. This period of opposition will be transcended.

THE IMAGE

Fire and water are opposite elements. They can never mingle. Thus does the Wise Leader preserve his individuality. He may live and work among the multitudes, but he is always a soul unto himself.

38. OPPOSITION

CHANGES

1. Stand still and a runaway horse will return of its own will. So will an estranged friend. If dealing with hostile people, avoid being hostile in return. Endure them.

2. An accidental meeting may bring estranged people together if their relationship is meant to be. It will be beneficial if you meet someone in this way.

3. It feels as if everything is conspiring against you. Do not be misled from your path. Stay on the path you know to be right and better fortune will follow.

4. You may face opposition from others, or self-doubt from within. If you meet someone in whom you can trust, you can overcome the sense of isolation you feel.

5. When you feel alone, it can be difficult to recognise a trustworthy person. When you do identify someone like this, work with them.

6. It is a mistake not to trust your friends. When it is regained, the tension will be resolved. When opposition reaches its climax, this is the time of its reversal.

39. OBSTRUCTION

Above: The Abysmal (Water)
Below: Keeping still (Mountain)

THE CONDITION

This hexagram represents an abyss before you, and a steep mountain rising behind you. You are surrounded by obstacles., To face the danger without you must be still within, like the mountain. By turning inward, your attention is directed to overcoming the obstacles.

THE JUDGEMENT

Obstructions are not overcome by pushing forward into danger, nor by doing nothing. One must retreat and prepare. Join with like-minded people, seek help from a leader, and keep your goal in mind. The obstruction is temporary, and a good vehicle for your personal development. This is the value of adversity. Learn from any errors and do not blame others.

THE IMAGE

Water at the top of the mountain cannot flow down because it is obstructed. Instead it collects and rises until it overflows the barrier. So does the Wise Leader raise her own inner being.

39. OBSTRUCTION

CHANGES

1. When first encountering an obstruction it is wise to reflect on how best to deal with it. Do not give up the struggle, but wait until a better time to act.

2. If you cannot go around a barrier, then you must confront it. There is no blame in confronting the obstacle directly if the cause is good and right.

3. You have a duty to others close to you. This duty is higher than the need to confront the obstacle. Others need you more. Retreat and care for them first.

4. You cannot confront the obstacle single handedly. You do not have the strength. You need the help of trustworthy companions overcome the obstacle.

5. In great adversity, friends will come. Your strength of spirit will attract valuable helpers. Working together, you will overcome the barriers.

6. If there are still obstacles, do not walk away from them. To go back and deal with them is the favoured course of action. Having a wise adviser will also bring fortune.

40. DELIVERANCE

Above: The Arousing (Thunder)
Below: The Abysmal (Water)

THE CONDITION

This Hexagram represents the movement away from danger. When the thunder has passed and the storm is over, the air is cleared. Tension is released. This is the first step in the movement however. The process of deliverance is beginning, it has not yet been fully achieved.

THE JUDGEMENT

When tensions begin to pass it is best to find your way back to a regular life as soon as possible. Beware that the feeling of liberation stemming from the release does not result in rashness of action. Do not push forward further than necessary. If there are any residual issues outstanding, deal with these as soon as possible. Make a clean sweep of things.

THE IMAGE

As thunderstorms pass, so does the Wise Leader allow the mistakes of others to pass. There is forgiveness and pardon, even for those who sinned willingly. Through her clarity comes deliverance.

40. DELIVERANCE

CHANGES

1. When the danger has passed or the obstacle overcome, take some time to rest and recuperate in peace. This will help order to return.

2. There are others being devious and cunning like foxes around you. To achieve deliverance they must be stopped. But this must be done rightly and with moderation.

3. Beware of taking your deliverance from being in need for granted. There will be disgrace if you flaunt your newly acquired good fortune or wealth.

4. In difficult times, lesser people can cling to the wise. When the time for deliverance comes, you must begin to free yourself of them. If not, true friends will mistrust you.

5. You must break free completely from the lesser people who have clung to you during the difficult times. It will take inner resolve, but you must remove yourself from them.

6. It may be necessary to use force to break out of the situation you have with people of lower qualities. Do so only when you are sure.

41. DECREASE

Above: Keeping still (Mountain)
Below: The Joyous (Lake)

THE CONDITION

This hexagram shows the lower Trigram losing a strong Yang line to the upper Trigram. If the foundations of a building are decreased in order to strengthen the upper floors, the building loses stability. However, decrease is not a bad thing if it means reducing what is too much.

THE JUDGEMENT

Decrease is natural, it comes in its own time. When money is scarce, thrift is no disgrace. If simplicity is what is needed, do not be ashamed, it helps build the inner resources needed for great undertakings. If anything you have to offer is given sincerely there is no humiliation. You do not have to present a false appearance to anyone.

THE IMAGE

Joy can increase into abandon, the strength of the mountain can turn to stubbornness. So the Wise Leader realises the need for decrease. Baseness is decreased, for higher nature to increase.

41. DECREASE

CHANGES

1. Beware that people that you may help do not become dependant on you. This would decrease them. Similarly, do not become dependant on a helper yourself or be too demanding of them.

2. Do not decrease yourself by submitting to the unreasonable demands of others. Do only what is reasonable and retain your dignity and self-respect.

3. Mistrust arise when a third person encroaches on two others. The trio must decrease by one. Only a pair can work.

4. Your own faults may be preventing others from getting closer and helping you. Stop your negative behaviour and they will be more inclined to make an approach. This will be to the good of all.

5. Fate is favouring you. You need not fear anything. You are to be increased. The time of decrease is about to pass.

6. With decrease passed, the time for increase will benefit all. Still you need to persevere and avoid acting for personal gain. Others can help and share the benefits.

42. INCREASE

Above: The Gentle (Wind)
Below: The Arousing (Thunder)

THE CONDITION

In this Hexagram the upper Trigram is giving a strong Yang line to the lower Trigram. It is sacrificing itself for the good of those below, who are increased by it. In terms of leadership, this is the great lesson. To lead truly is to serve. This is a time of enlightenment and clarity.

THE JUDGEMENT

When people in power make sacrifices, the people below are filled with gratitude and joy. There is a general sense of well-being. In such times, difficult ventures can be undertaken and existing tasks can make good progress. This spirit of enthusiasm and achievement cannot last, it will pass naturally like a season. Make the most of it and get things done.

THE IMAGE

As the thunder and the wind increase and strengthen each other, so the Wise Leader increases his own personality by imitating the good in others. If he sees something bad in himself, he removes it.

42. INCREASE

CHANGES

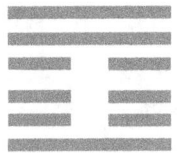

1. This is good time to use your increased strength or authority to achieve something that you may not have believed yourself to be capable of. Do it selflessly and you will succeed.

2. When you do the right thing at the right time, success will follow naturally. You do not have to force anything. But beware of letting success detract you from the good.

3. If you act with honour and sincerity, even misfortune will help you increase your inner strength. You will learn from it.

4. If you find yourself in the middle of people above and people below, use the opportunity serve both sides equally. In this position you can have a great influence on the outcome.

5. If you act with a truly kind heart, you will receive the greatest of rewards. Not prestige or fame, but recognition of being wise and good and worthy.

6. If you do not act to help others increase you will lose influence and be open to criticism. This is a time for giving, not taking.

43. BREAKTHROUGH

Above: The Joyous (Lake)
Below: The Creative (Heaven)

THE CONDITION

This Hexagram represents a breakthrough after a long period of increasing tension. The dark line at the top of the Hexagram indicates that the negative influence of others is waning. In such times of breakthrough, a surge of strength can change things for the better.

THE JUDGEMENT

Where there conflict between good and evil, or rationality and passion, a struggle must ensue. If you need to fight you must resolve the conflict with strength, but also goodwill. Do not use direct force. Evil has greater force. Do not compromise. To prevail, discredit evil, especially that which lies within yourself. Fight against evil by fighting for the good.

THE IMAGE

When the lake has evaporated into clouds, you can expect a cloudburst. Thus the Wise Leader distributes her riches and resources as she goes along. There is no build up of tension in first place.

43. BREAKTHROUGH

CHANGES

1. You feel inspired to press forward, but resistance is still strong. Do not over-reach yourself. At this early stage of breaking through, a setback could be disastrous.

2. Be resolute in your action to push ahead, but be very cautious too. Look ahead and be alert for the unexpected. As you begin to succeed, the negative forces with withdraw.

3. Someone near you may not be trustworthy. Beware of cutting them loose too quickly. They might become even more disruptive. Endure for now and wait for the right time.

4. Pushing forward against the advice of others is just obstinacy. The obstacles are too great. If you refuse to listen you will fail.

5. Dealing with the evil around you is like clearing weeds. They can quickly grow back. The conflict is not hopeless. You will succeed if you persevere.

6. Evil does not die easily. Just when you think you are victorious, evil can reappear. Stay on guard. Be thorough and avoid carelessness. If you overlook an important detail, the evil may rise again.

44. COMING TO MEET

Above: The Creative (Heaven)
Below: The Gentle (Wind)

THE CONDITION

This Hexagram represents a dark force that was thought to be eliminated, but has entered the scene again from within, and below. It is like the days growing shorter after the summer solstice. The situation is dangerous. You must act to prevent misfortune.

THE JUDGEMENT

There is danger of being taken in by an inferior person. By meeting with the inferior who comes to you, you can give them power. They do not seem dangerous, but they are. There is a beneficial way of coming to meet with an inferior. It is when they meet half-way with freedom from dishonesty or ulterior motives. If this is not the case, harm will follow.

THE IMAGE

Heaven sends the wind to produce motion on the earth. When distant from the population, the Wise Leader sends words and messages to set things in motion and to keep order.

44. COMING TO MEET

CHANGES

1. Beware of danger that lies within. A weak pig can eat and become dangerous. You must check for any inferior elements. Beware of underestimating their potential for danger.

2. When an evil element is identified, control it by gentle means. To a pig, a pen is a home, not a prison. Once in check, keep it there. Do not let it escape to do evil.

3. Beware of being tempted by what the inferior element is offering. Keep aware of the dangers and you will avoid them.

4. Do not turn your back on the people below you. Do not become too aloof to realise that if you alienate yourself from them, they will not be there when you need them.

5. Look after people properly and they will look after you when you need them. Tolerate and protect those who may follow you. They will fall like ripe fruit to help you, but a fruit that ripens of its own will.

6. Your actions may lead you to being disliked. If the people who dislike you are inferior, bear it with composure

45. GATHERING TOGETHER

Above: The Joyous (Lake)
Below: The Receptive (Earth)

THE CONDITION

This Hexagram represents devotion within and joyousness without. It is the basis for the coming together of people. They may gather naturally as a family, or by other means like that of working together. Like a lake is a gathering of water, this is about the gathering of people.

THE JUDGEMENT

This is a time of integration for the family or the group that is brought together. There is a spirituality generated by the gathering and the spiritual nature is strong. There must also be a self aware and collected leader around whom the others can unite. The undertaking of great deeds is favoured with the union of devotion and joy.

THE IMAGE

As a lake may overflow, the gathering of many people may cause difficulties. The Wise Leader is aware of the dangers and is prepared for the unexpected. If forearmed, problems can be prevented.

45. GATHERING TOGETHER

CHANGES

1. Without a leader there may be confusion and wavering. Yet the response of the leader to a cry for help brings great joy and laughter.

2. Natural forces are at work to bring people together who need to be together. If the need for meeting and joining is sincere, successful bonds will be made.

3. Joining with a group will be favourable. If it means swallowing some pride and asking someone to help you become a member of it, so be it. This will not be a mistake.

4. Now is the time to work towards achieving unity amongst others, rather than rewards for oneself. Being selfless will bring greater rewards.

5. A leader may have high rank, but this alone is not enough to earn respect. This can only be achieved by the leader's steadfast devotion to duty.

6. You may have sought the alliance of another but a misunderstanding has caused difficulties. Explaining how you feel may enable them to see more clearly.

46. PUSHING UPWARD

Above: The Receptive (Earth)
Below: The Gentle (Wood)

THE CONDITION

This hexagram represents wood growing within the earth and pushing upward. This kind of movement is not achieved easily. Effort and willpower are needed. Such effort needs to be in harmony with the situation. You must begin at the bottom and work your way up.

THE JUDGEMENT

The time is right for success to be achieved by being modest and adaptable, not harsh or violent. Seeking the advice of others will also be beneficial. Almost anything you do will work towards your advancement. It is the right time for action. You are favoured by fate. Make the most of this time, it will not last forever.

THE IMAGE

As wood grows slowly within the earth, so the Wise Leader makes steady and continuous progress, bending around obstacles and adapting when necessary to the conditions.

46. PUSHING UPWARD

CHANGES

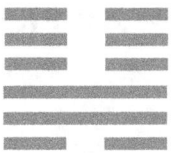

1. From being in a lowly position, the time has come to start an ascent. Your power comes from knowing what it is like to start from humble beginnings.

2. You may feel that what you have to offer is insufficient to gain the attention of those above you. This is not the case. If you are sincere and upright, it will be noticed.

3. Obstructions to your progress wither away. It is the good luck that fate provides. Do not question it. Make the most of it but do not rely upon it for the future.

4. The attainment of all you wanted is to hand. Do not waste the achievement. Use it to foster the well-being of others. Do this and your efforts will endure.

5. Beware of becoming intoxicated by success. Keep taking things one step at a time. Only calm and steady progress will lead to the final goal. Persevere.

6. Do not push blindly onward for its own sake. This will just lead to exhaustion. Remember where you really want to be, and act consistently with this.

47. OPPRESSION

Above: The Joyous (Lake)
Below: The Abysmal (Water)

THE CONDITION

This Hexagram represents a lake that has dried up and is exhausted. An abyss has been opened within the lake and the water has gone. This is an exceptional time when great people are oppressed and restrained by inferior people. Fate and chance have brought a time of adversity.

THE JUDGEMENT

This is a time that will test your character. If you confront difficulties with good cheer, your character will be strengthened for later success. But there will be no success if your spirit breaks in the face of adversity. People will be against you. Your words will not be believed. You will have no influence. Stay blameless and correct and you will see it through.

THE IMAGE

When the lake is exhausted, the Wise Leader accepts the oppression of the time and sees it through, remaining true to themselves at the deepest level. Only this can overcome the external circumstances.

47. OPPRESSION

CHANGES

1. When adversity strikes, remain strong within. If not, you will be overcome. If you sit and do nothing, you will not succeed. Keep moving along the path.

2. You have the essentials of life, but you are not content. You are oppressing yourself inwardly. Try to gain some inner preparation before taking action.

3. You are restless and indecisive. Even minor obstacles seem insurmountable. You may be relying on what is inherently unstable. Seek to be firmer in your resolution.

4. The comfort you currently enjoy is oppressing your inner nature to do good for others. Your activity is slowed, but with willpower you can overcome the impasse.

5. You are seeking others to help you in your venture, but no helpers are to be found. Be patient and remain calm. Stay composed and things will improve.

6. Your bonds of oppression are soon to be broken. Forget the recent difficult past. Do not let it hinder your actions. Lose your fear and act decisively.

48. THE WELL

Above: The Abysmal (Water)
Below: The Gentle (Wood)

THE CONDITION

This hexagram represents a well with wooden pole descending into water to raise it up. Thus it describes an inexhaustible source of nourishment. In human terms, it represents the continuing nature of the deep human need of living within a structured society.

THE JUDGEMENT

To achieve a lasting social structure, or other enduring effects, you must go beyond the superficial and meet the deeper human needs. You must act carefully, and with sensitivity. No matter what social hierarchy may exist, all people are of the same essential nature. All can draw from the divine in themselves as long as they are neither shallow nor careless.

THE IMAGE

As a plant draws up water to give itself nourishment and life, so does the Wise Leader encourage people to help one another. Thus all the various parts cooperate for the benefit of the whole.

48. THE WELL

CHANGES

1. There is only mud at the bottom of your well. You are not sustaining yourself. Do not throw yourself away. No one will care for you if you do not care for yourself.

2. You have fine qualities, but you neglect to nurture them and they have deteriorated. Your well is not used. No one comes to draw water from it.

3. Your well is clear, but no-one drinks from it. Your talents are not being utilised. If someone in authority knew what you can offer, things would be better.

4. You are recognising that you have things about yourself to put in order. Your well is being lined and repaired. Although it is out of use now. It will bring sustenance later.

5. Your well is clear and fed by a fresh stream. The water needs to be brought to the surface for others to drink. You have the skills and talent to do good. Use them.

6. You have great inner wealth. Your well is clear and there is no hindrance to those who drink from it. The more they take, the greater your wealth. You are a blessing.

49. REVOLUTION

Above: The Joyous (Lake)
Below: The Clinging (Fire)

THE CONDITION

This hexagram represents fire within a lake. These elements are in direct conflict and so there is revolution. The seasons change, and the changes make demands on people. When nations, regimes and people change, other fundamental changes are necessary.

THE JUDGEMENT

Revolution is a last resort that must never be decided upon lightly. It must be with the will of the people, and at the correct and crucial time. It must be done for the benefit of the people. It must be done without selfish motives. It must be done to meet a real need to replace chaos with stability. Only in this way can it be instigated out without remorse.

THE IMAGE

The seasons change and bring revolutions. The Wise Leader uses her knowledge of nature to prepare for such times. Thus she can bring clarity and order into times of chaos and extreme changes.

49. REVOLUTION

CHANGES

1. Do not act prematurely. The time for action has yet to arrive. You must exercise self-restraint. Be firm. Hold fire or misfortune will follow.

2. There is much preparation to do before instigating any drastic action. Inner preparation must come first. Ensure there is a leader who will be followed and trusted.

3. The right time must be chosen with care. It is easy to act with too much haste, or with too much hesitation. Make sure there is no viable alternative course of action.

4. Your cause must be just and founded on a higher truth if others are to support you. You must have the inner strength as well as the outer authority to act and lead the way.

5. You must communicate your intentions and instructions clearly and truthfully. For others to follow and act in the correct spirit, they need clear guidance.

6. Once the fundamental change has happened, more detailed reforms need to be carried out. Do not push too hard for these however. Just do what is feasible.

50. THE GREAT BOWL

Above: The Clinging (Fire)
Below: The Gentle (Wood / Wind)

THE CONDITION

This hexagram represents a fire lit under a great bronze bowl that was used by cultured families to cook and serve food to honoured guests. It it also symbolic of establishing something new after the old has been abolished. Something new comes from existing ingredients.

THE JUDGEMENT

Wood nourishes fire as the spirit of life. There is great good fortune. The wise and good people must be nourished in order complete their tasks. This is a time for finishing what has been started. People who are leaders must set out what needs to be done with clarity and firmness. This is also a time for others to start climbing the ladder to a higher position.

THE IMAGE

The wood within the fire gives power to the flame. So the Wise Leader fuels and renews her inner flame with gentleness, but also with firmness when necessary. In this way comes prosperity for all.

50. THE GREAT BOWL

CHANGES

1. In a good society, all people can succeed and achieve good things no matter how lowly they may be. If you can prove yourself, you will attain recognition.

2. Your bowl contains good food. You are succeeding. This may cause envy and resentment in others. Continue as you are. Do not get entangled with the envious.

3. Your progress is blocked. You may be working on something wonderful, but it cannot be completed. Remain calm. Keep your patience and the blockage will pass.

4. You are being unrealistic in your expectations. You cannot achieve if you have great plans but little knowledge, or great responsibility but little power.

5. Maintain a balanced approach to the situation. Seek advice from wise people and approach them with modesty. Be open and receptive to what they say.

6. Like the jade ring on the cauldron, be firm yet gentle. The adviser and the leader are complementary. Good fortune will follow.

51. THE AROUSING

Above: The Arousing (Thunder)
Below: The Arousing (Thunder)

THE CONDITION

This Hexagram represents forceful, and fearful upwards movement. It is the shock and terror of violent thunder, doubled. Thunderstorms in Spring herald the awakening of new life. In human terms, someone has become prominent by the use of great power and force.

THE JUDGEMENT

There has been a great shock. There is fear. But fear makes us cautious and careful, and this leads to good fortune. If you have experienced great fear in the past, you can use the experience to protect you now and in the future. Remain composed in spirit despite the thunder. Concentration is needed in doing things correctly. In this way no harm will come.

THE IMAGE

The Wise Leader can know fear and trembling as well as anyone else. But he uses this to examine his own reactions, and to learn from them. In this way does he learn to shape his life and put it in order.

51. THE AROUSING

CHANGES

1. After the shock and the fear of the first thunder, there is relief. There may even be laughter once the shock has passed. In due course fear brings good fortune.

2. If you have suffered losses. This must be accepted. Do not seek to resist or fight back. What was lost will be regained. Withdraw for now.

3. In times of shock it can be easy to lose your presence of mind. Do not overlook the opportunity to act. This is a time to stir yourself inwardly to overcome the blows.

4. The shock has confused you. You have been knocked off balance. You feel incapable to act. You need to become clear about what you need to do and make a decision.

5. You receive one shock after another. There seems to be no escaping the constant blows. Conserve your strength. Behave correctly. This will provide some stability.

6. The terrible events are at their height. If it is impossible to act with any presence of mind, keep as still as possible. Don't let other people's panic infect you. Withdraw.

52. KEEPING STILL

Above: Keeping still (Mountain)
Below: Keeping still (Mountain)

THE CONDITION

This hexagram represents being at rest. It is the rest that comes when movement has reached its natural end. It is the rest that promotes stillness and meditation. It is not easy to attain a quiet heart. But it is vital to prepare one's mind and spirit for future ventures.

THE JUDGEMENT

Rest and movement must be in accord with the time. Sitting with one's back straight, the lotus position replicates the mountain. In this way can you become calm. Ego and personality dissolve in the stillness. Once inner calm has been achieved, you can see the world in a different light. In such inner stillness action is intuitive. No mistakes are made.

THE IMAGE

The mountain keeps still within itself. As does the Wise Leader who sees and feels as each moment demands. Not in worry for the future, nor in regret for the past. Her will does not stray.

52. KEEPING STILL

CHANGES

1. With the intuitive knowledge of innocence, you are aware of the reality of the situation and can stop yourself going in a wrong direction before you even begin.

2. Someone above you is heading in the wrong direction. If your warnings are ignored you cannot save them. Keep still. Following will bring unhappiness.

3. Do not force stillness upon yourself. True stillness does not come from rigidity or great effort. Allow calmness to come naturally from inner composure.

4. You have yet to reach the highest state of peace and stillness. The dangers of doubt and unrest remain within you. This is not a bad thing. In time stillness will be achieved.

5. Keep your mouth still. Beware of being too free with your words. Ill spoken words may bring trouble. Choose your words carefully and have no regrets.

6. When you have reached the state of true rest, you can be at ease with both the trivial and the important issues of life. True stillness holds for every individual situation.

53. DEVELOPMENT

Above: The Gentle (Wood / Wind)
Below: Keeping still (Mountain)

THE CONDITION

This Hexagram represents a tree that grows on a mountain. It develops slowly, but also becomes deeply and firmly rooted. In human terms it shows the way for gradual development - stillness and tranquility within, deep penetration and long life without.

THE JUDGEMENT

Gradual development is the correct way for ventures that require cooperation. Hasty action is not wise and any formalities need to be adhered to. Within oneself, development should also follow a gradual course to achieve lasting results. One must cultivate inner calm, for when this is combined with adaptability and perseverance it is a great source of progress.

THE IMAGE

Like a tree on a mountain, the Wise Leader is visible from afar and is an example to all. Influence and weight can only come through constant and gradual personal development. A slow process.

53. DEVELOPMENT

CHANGES

1. When you are just starting a new venture, you can be lonely, without help, and surrounded by strangers. Yet, it is these very difficulties that prevent haste and actually help you to make progress.

2. You take a step further when initial insecurity is overcome, and confidence begins to grow. Be ready to share your good fortune with others.

3. If you push rashly into a struggle, misfortune will follow. Maintain your position, but do not provoke conflict.

4. You may be in a situation where it is difficult to keep out of danger. Be sensible and yielding. Find a refuge, where you can keep out of harm's way for a while.

5. You may find that someone closest to you has misjudged or misunderstood you. This has hindered progress. In time the misunderstanding will pass and you will be reconciled.

6. The work is completed. Something great has been achieved. There is now a shining example for others to follow.

54. THE MARRYING MAIDEN

Above: The Arousing (Thunder)
Below: The Joyous (Lake)

THE CONDITION

This hexagram represents a joyous maiden who enters the family of the partner of her choice. It is about the nature of relationships. These Trigrams are also associated with spring and autumn, encompassing the beginning and the end of the cycle of life.

THE JUDGEMENT

A person who newly joins a family or group ca bring tension and disorder. There is no contractual agreement, so tact, caution and reserve are needed if the relationships are to flourish. As yet, the new person has no power or authority. Trying to move forward will not bring favourable results. There must also be the most uniting factor of all: love.

THE IMAGE

Thunder stirs the surface of a lake. Relationships are always in danger of misunderstandings and arguments. The Wise Leader remains focused on the everlasting relationship, and avoids the pitfalls.

54. THE MARRYING MAIDEN

CHANGES

1. Someone new to a family or group must learn how to fit in with the pattern of its life. Until confidence is built, it is best to stay modestly in the background.

2. Someone key to the group may have gone away. Though you may feel disappointed at this, do not let it affect your sense of loyalty. Be faithful to your duty.

3. Do not throw yourself into a group that you are not certain about just for the sake of it. If you enter into a role that you are not compatible with, no joy will come of it.

4. It is wise and virtuous to wait until you are certain that you are joining a group for the right reasons. It may take a longer time, but your patience will be rewarded.

5. You may need to adapt yourself to a new group situation. Do not put on any airs and graces. You may have higher credentials but you should concentrate on doing your duty.

6. If a group is joined, commitment needs to be shown. If this is not done, there can be no respect. A group or family with just a superficial affinity will not prosper.

55. ABUNDANCE

Above: The Arousing (Thunder)
Below: The Clinging (Fire)

THE CONDITION

This hexagram represents thunder and lightening joining together in a show of power. A climax is indicated. There is clarity of vision, and strength of action. Together these can bring about greatness of achievement, and prosperity. There is abundance.

THE JUDGEMENT

There is a time of abundance. But such times are naturally brief. When something has reached a peak, the only way is down. However, there is no need for premature sadness. Make the most of the abundance and enjoy it while it is here. Use the current time to establish firm social, spiritual and financial foundations for the future.

THE IMAGE

Thunder and lightening together. Inner clarity and outward action. This is a time for the enforcement of the law. Inner clarity to investigate for truth. Outward action to enforce just penalties.

55. ABUNDANCE

CHANGES

1. Seeking out someone to help you in your work will work towards achieving abundance. But beware of the partnership lasting for longer than is necessary.

2. Your good work is being eclipsed by someone's plotting and intrigue. Taking countermeasures will only make things worse. Continue without fuss and your work will be noticed .

3. People of low ability are pushing themselves into positions of influence. Continue to work but take no action. Remain blameless

4. Your work is at last being recognised. You can now forge ahead with wisdom and energy. These are the complementary forces that will now unite to produce abundance.

5. A good leader is modest and open to the views of others. Thus she is surrounded by able people who work towards achievements that benefit all people. Success is near.

6. He who seeks abundance and fame with arrogance and self-interest will achieve the opposite. He will alienate even his own family and enjoy only isolation and misery.

56. THE WANDERER

Above: The Clinging (Fire)
Below: Keeping still (Mountain)

THE CONDITION

This Hexagram represents fires burning on a mountainside. The fires are blown by the wind from place to place. Thus the image of the wanderer; a traveller who is separate and cannot find a place to settle. Although reserved, he is steadfast and achieves good fortune.

THE JUDGEMENT

The wanderer achieves success through being cautious and reserved. Being helpful and obliging to others protects him from evil. The wanderer who is unpretentious cannot be humiliated even though he is constantly in the company of new people in strange lands. It is a great thing to truly understand the inner meaning of the wanderer.

THE IMAGE

Fire on the mountain does not tarry. Cases in law should also be like this, not dragged out indefinitely. Prison too should be a temporary lodging place, not a permanent dwelling.

56. THE WANDERER

CHANGES

1. A wanderer does not waste time on trivialities. Be humble on the outside, but retain your inner dignity. You will not find friends by playing the fool.

2. Whist modest, the wanderer still shows love for others. People warm to him. Such a way of being can attract people who will be faithful friends and helpers.

3. Wanderers must beware of behaving badly. Meddling can bring misfortune. Arrogance can lose the support and loyalty of others. This puts him in great danger.

4. The wanderer's inner strength and virtue will always help him obtain shelter. But he is not immune to danger. He must stay on his guard, always aware that he is a stranger.

5. At times the wander may settle for a while. What he has to offer will be readily accepted. He can settle in a strange land if he knows how to adapt to the way of things.

6. If the wanderer is not careful or prudent, misfortune will follow. Laughter can turn sour if he forgets that he is still a stranger. He must not lose his modesty.

57. THE GENTLE

Above: The Gentle (Wind / Wood)
Below: The Gentle (Wind / Wood)

THE CONDITION

This Hexagram represents gentleness and adaptability, but also penetration. The wind penetrates all places on earth, and roots penetrate below the earth. In the sky, the wind moves dark clouds. So the gentle force can disperse dark forces and enable the hidden to be seen.

THE JUDGEMENT

Gentleness succeeds when the goal is clear. It achieves through small, continuous and consistent influences. Results are less noticeable but they endure for longer. Having a good ally will also help. Whilst remaining in the background, you can achieve great things by taking gentle steps, fuelled by gaining a deep understanding of the situation, and being flexible.

THE IMAGE

Like the ceaseless wind, the Wise Leader penetrates the soul of the people and blows away the clouds that hide evil. Her influence is lasting as it comes from enlightenment. Her commands are obeyed.

57. THE GENTLE

CHANGES

1. Like the ceaseless wind, the Wise Leader penetrates the soul of the people and blows away the clouds that hide evil. Her influence is lasting as it comes from enlightenment. Her commands are obeyed.

2. There are hidden influences against you. Trace them back to their roots and bring them to light. If you do this, their powers will be lost. The effort will be worth it.

3. Once you have reflected on all of the major considerations and made up your mind to act, do it. Continuous reflection will only bring further doubt and exhaustion.

4. There will be good fortune if you combine modesty and gentleness with energy and action. There is much merit in the person who can wield such attributes.

5. Be steadfast in your actions. Beforehand, ponder well on the potential outcomes. After taking action reflect again on the actual results and continue act correctly.

6. If you are working against darker forces, beware of getting too involved with them. Make sure you have the energy to combat them. Beware of losing yourself.

58. THE JOYOUS

Above: The Joyous (Lake)
Below: The Joyous (Lake)

THE CONDITION

This Hexagram represents a smiling lake, doubled. The lake refreshes and brings joy. The yielding line at the top of each Trigram symbolises a gentle and joyful personality. The two lines beneath represent strength. Thus there is a doubling of joy without and strength within.

THE JUDGEMENT

Joy is infectious can help achieve great things. But it must be steadfast and not degenerate into superficial mirth. The person who has inner strength and outer gentleness can build worthwhile and lasting relationships. People's hearts are won through friendship. They will support the leader and each with great loyalty. This is the best way of leading people.

THE IMAGE

Two lakes joined will replenish each other. So does the Wise Leader join with others to discuss matters and learn from every participant. Thus learning comes from all people cheerfully and joyously.

58. THE JOYOUS

CHANGES

1. You can be content with life as it is. Let doubts and concerns be distant from you. Be free of selfishness and become blessed with inner security and joy.

2. Beware of being drawn in to inappropriate pleasures and base amusements. This will bring remorse. Remain sincere and steadfast and maintain others' respect.

3. True joy comes from within. If you are empty within, all pleasures will be mere indulgences. These will eventually overwhelm you ad you will lose yourself.

4. If you need to make choices between higher or lower pleasures, you have no inner peace, only suffering. Decide on what will give you true joy and follow that path.

5. Beware of being drawn in by unworthy influences. Evil can creep up slowly if you are not aware. Recognise the danger and protect yourself.

6. Lose your vanity or you will succumb to base pleasures that will control you. Regain your integrity and direction in life. Stop depending on external influences.

59. DISPERSION

Above: The Gentle (Wind)
Below: The Abysmal (Water)

THE CONDITION

This Hexagram represents wind blowing over water and dispersing the ice of winter and also the dispersion of clouds which then allows the sun to shine through. In human terms, it represents the dispersion of anger, resentment and frustration within others or oneself.

THE JUDGEMENT

People are divided and blocked by egotism and negativity. A leader should now strive for unity. There was joy, but this has now been dispersed. There have been hardships more recently, and now these too will be dispersed. Achieving unity will be difficult, but action should not be forced. Disperse the clouds gently and the sun will come through on its own.

THE IMAGE

Spring's warm winds blow steadily across the waters and stir the ice of winter. The Wise Leader helps people make connections with what is of true value to them, and unites them in a common cause.

59. DISPERSION

CHANGES

1. When you see the beginning of disunity, act quickly to disperse it. Deal with any misunderstandings. Like the wind, dispel the clouds before they can gather into a storm.

2. Any feeling of alienation from others should be dealt with. Do not act in anger. Be moderate and calm. Dissolve the ill-will with gentleness and objectivity.

3. Put aside personal desires and direct your will towards completing your task. Disperse your inner barriers, think not of yourself, and success will follow.

4. When carrying out great work for the good of others, even your friends may need to be set aside temporarily. Take the wider view. Forego what is near to win what is far.

5. When people are needed to help achieve a venture, a new idea can provide a focal point for rallying assistance. A different approach may break the deadlock.

6. Danger is at hand. If necessary, you may need to retreat or escape from it. You may also need to save others. There is no blame in this. Avoiding danger is not a mistake.

60. LIMITATION

Above: The Abysmal (Water)
Below: The Joyous (Lake)

THE CONDITION

This Hexagram represents the limitations of a lake. Unlike water in general, which is inexhaustible, a lake can overflow if too much water enters it. In human terms it represents the limits that people must set for themselves in their actions, thoughts and even finances.

THE JUDGEMENT

Setting limitations to our lives can be tiresome, but also valuable. Limitations to our spending are necessary to ensure we do not want. Limitations of powers are also necessary to regulate and prevent abuse. However, limitations should not be set too stringently. Too much self limitation can bring unhappiness. Too much limitation on others can bring revolt.

THE IMAGE

The lake limits what is otherwise inexhaustible. So the Wise Leader sets limits to what would otherwise become a life without boundaries. She is aware that self-limitation is the basis of freedom.

60. LIMITATION

CHANGES

1. If things are progressing beyond your ability to cope, then you must stop. Wait until your position has strengthened. Recognise your limits.

2. When the time for action arrives do not hesitate. Act. When obstacles are present, it is right to wait. But when they are overcome, anxiety and hesitation will lead to misfortune.

3. Do not blame others for your own lack of self-control. Realise your own mistakes. Set your own limits wisely. Excess brings regret.

4. The limitations you set yourself must not be too stringent. They should come naturally and without undue effort. Be adaptable to change. Avoid vain struggles.

5. Beware of setting limitations for others that you do not follow yourself. This provokes resentment and resistance. Limit yourself first. Lead by example.

6. People will rebel against unacceptably harsh restrictions. Your body will also react negatively to unnatural limitations. Enforce limitations only if they help you grow.

61. INNER TRUTH

Above: The Gentle (Wind)
Below: The Joyous (Lake)

THE CONDITION

This hexagram represents the invisible force of the wind blowing over a lake, stirring its surface. The Inner Truth is such a force. The centre shows a humble heart, open to the truth. The basis of great achievement is here too: loyalty to those above, and gentleness to those below.

THE JUDGEMENT

The force of inner truth must grow great before it can influence those who are obstinate or intractable. The secret is to find the right approach. Seek to understand the truth within the difficult person. Only when this door has been opened can you to begin to influence them. If the bond is based upon what is right, no obstacle is insurmountable.

THE IMAGE

The Wise Leader aims to penetrate the minds of wrongdoers to gain a sympathetic understanding of their circumstances. The kind of understanding that knows how to pardon leaves a deep impression.

61. INNER TRUTH

CHANGES

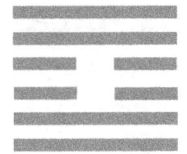

1. The force of inner truth depends upon inner stability. Beware of making secret bonds with others. It will bring anxiety and the inner truth will be lost.

2. When you voice your feelings openly and honestly, their influence will be far-reaching. Do not strive for this to happen or the effect will be destroyed.

3. If the source of your strength lies in relationships with others, be prepared to be swung from joy to sorrow. You must decide if this is a good or bad way to be.

4. Perhaps it is time to seek support from a wiser, more experienced person. It may take some strength to turn away from immediate friends, to this wiser person.

5. By personality, you can unite those around you. Inner truth is needed to be able to do this rightly, otherwise the unity is a deception.

6. You may have achieved much, but to crow about it like a cockerel, not just at dawn, but all day invites misfortune. Do not exaggerate your successes.

62. GREAT SMALLNESS

Above: The Arousing (Thunder)
Below: Keeping still (Mountain)

THE CONDITION

This Hexagram represents an exceptional time of transition. Here, two strong lines are enclosed by four weak lines. There is a danger of flying too far from the ground and losing touch with reality. An authority figure is inadequate for the task. Great care is needed.

THE JUDGEMENT

This exceptional time demands great modesty and conscientious service. This must not be done in too servile or obsequious a manner, but with inner dignity. Do not count on success. There is insufficient strength to succeed. This is not a time to push forward any ambitions. Any attempt to gain great things will fail. Only small things can be gained in these times.

THE IMAGE

Thunder rages over the mountain. The Wise Leader is aware of the time and restricts his actions to conducting his duty. He aligns himself with the lowly, showing humility and frugality.

62.

CHANGES

1. The is danger when self-restraint is abandoned. Trying to soar like a bird will bring misfortune. Flying up at the wrong time puts the bird in sight of the hunter.

2. Great restraint is needed. Accept the situation if you can only achieve a lower goal. Do not use force to achieve anything. Just complete your duties conscientiously.

3. Beware of over-confidence. Just when you think you are safe, something evil will take you by surprise. These are exceptional times. Pay attention to detail.

4. There is a temptation to take the initiative and act. Do not. This will lead to danger. Keep inwardly strong and steadfast to avoid mistakes.

5. There is the prospect of a change for the better arriving. But it is not here yet. The right people need to be chosen to help the positive transition begin.

6. If you do not know when to stop, you will career onwards to destruction. This is arrogance. This is not the time for flying high. Like an exhausted bird you will fall.

63. AFTER COMPLETION

Above: The Abysmal (Water)
Below: The Clinging (Fire)

THE CONDITION

This hexagram represents the achievement of order and cultural flowering after the completion of a difficult transition. Everything is in its proper place, and there is equilibrium. Yet it is also a time of caution, as any movement may cause imbalance and disorder to return.

THE JUDGEMENT

Most of what can be achieved has been achieved. All that remains to be done relates to small details. Such details are important though and should not be underestimated. Final success has not been fully realised until these details have been taken care of. Do not sit back and relax yet. Decay and misfortune await if caution is not maintained.

THE IMAGE

Water in a kettle over a fire. A need for balance. Too much water boils over and puts out the fire. Too much heat and the water will evaporate. The Wise Leader recognises danger and acts to avoid it.

63. AFTER COMPLETION

CHANGES

1. Others may be putting you under pressure to achieve more. This is not good. Do not succumb. Check what you are doing. If your behaviour is correct, no harm will ensue.

2. Those in higher positions may not be fostering your talent enough. Don't throw yourself at them. Wait. Stay calm. Develop inner strength and success will come.

3. In times of order, sights can be set too quickly on expansion. This will be dangerous, especially if you employ people who do not have the necessary abilities.

4. Hidden evils may become uncovered. Do not let the apparent success of the moment blind you to them. Do not neglect ill omens or you will not avert the consequences.

5. Great achievements can bring on great displays of success. Such displays are superficial and dangerous. Keep to simplicity. Do not endanger your inner worth.

6. A peril has been overcome but do not look back with self admiration. This will bring misfortune. Look ahead to new things and go forward.

64. BEFORE COMPLETION

Above: The Clinging (Fire)
Below: The Abysmal (Water)

THE CONDITION

This hexagram represents a time of change form disorder and danger, to order and clarity. The change however is not yet complete. It is like spring: a transitional period between the darkness of winter and the brightness and fruitfulness of summer.

THE JUDGEMENT

This is a difficult time. It is not easy to lead the world from darkness to light. It is a great responsibility. Success can be yours as long as you are deliberate and cautious. Be like an old fox crossing a frozen river. Use your ears to listen for the cracking of the ice and seek a safe route. Do not be like the young fox, bounding-in and getting his tail wet!

THE IMAGE

Fire and water are opposites in nature. The Wise Leader is aware of their different properties and uses her knowledge to make use of them. To use them correctly, she must first be correct in herself.

64. BEFORE COMPLETION

CHANGES

1. It is tempting to act quickly to achieve change. The time is not yet right. Over-enthusiasm will bring danger. Don't be like the young fox and get your tail wet.

2. The time to act has still not arrived. Be patient. Develop your inner strength to help you go forward when the time is right. Do not lose sight of the goal. Just wait.

3. The time has come to act, but you have yet to gain all the strength you will need. Forcing your way ahead will fail. Obtain help from others before stepping forward.

4. The time of struggle has arrived. To achieve the change you must be strong. Do not doubt yourself. You fight for good. You are laying the foundations for the future.

5. You have won a victory. You have overcome doubts and misgivings. You have helped turn winter into summer. People are happy to follow your light. A new time has arrived.

6. It is time to celebrate the bright new age. But do not overdo it. Get drunk on success and you will spoil the blessing.

www.ingramcontent.com/pod-product-compliance
Lightning Source LLC
Chambersburg PA
CBHW060858170526
45158CB00001B/402